INSIGHT GUIDES

NEW YORK
StepbyStep

APA PUBLICATIONS L

Part of the Langenscheidt Publishing Group

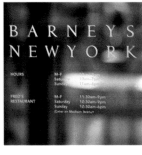

CONTENTS

ABOUT THIS BOOK

Above from top: the Stars and Stripes on Liberty Island; a quiet moment in Central Park; a view of Lower Manhattan; a New York tour bus; a Chelsea gallery.

This *Step by Step Guide* has been produced by the editors of Insight Guides, whose books have set the standard for visual travel guides since 1970. With top-quality photography and authoritative recommendations, this guidebook brings you the very best of New York in a series of 18 tailor-made tours.

WALKS AND TOURS

The tours in the book provide something to suit all budgets, tastes and trip lengths. As well as covering New York's many classic attractions, the tours track lesser-known sights and up-and-coming areas, as well as the city's outer boroughs of Brooklyn and the Bronx.

The tours embrace a range of interests, so whether you are an art fan, a movie buff, a gourmet, a shopaholic, or have kids to entertain, you will find an option to suit.

We recommend that you read the whole of a tour before setting out. This should help you to familiarize yourself with the route and enable you to plan where to stop for refreshments –

options for this are shown in the 'Food and Drink' boxes, recognizable by the knife and fork sign, on most pages.

For our pick of the tours by theme, consult Recommended Tours For… *(see pp.6–7)*.

ORIENTATION

The tours are set in context by this introductory section, giving an overview of the city to set the scene, plus background information on food and drink and shopping. A succinct history timeline in this chapter highlights the key events that have shaped New York over the centuries.

DIRECTORY

Also supporting the tours is a Directory chapter, comprising a user-friendly, clearly organized A–Z of practical information, our pick of where to stay while you are in the city, and select restaurant listings; these eateries complement the more low-key cafés and restaurants that feature within the tours themselves and are intended to offer a wider choice for evening dining.

The Author

This edition was revised and updated by Eleanor Berman, a New Yorker since 1981. Eleanor is the author of 14 travel guides, including two award-winning books on the city.

Original writer John Gattuso is the editor of Stone Creek Publications, as well as a veteran of more than a dozen Insight Guides. Born and raised in the New York metropolitan area, John first got to know the city as a boy on outings with his grandmother, whose sentiment 'There's nothing like New York,' the adult Gattuso wholly endorses.

The work of several other writers appears in this book, including frequent Insight contributors Edward A. Jardim, William Scheller, Kathy Novak, and Divya Symmers.

Margin Tips

Shopping tips, historical facts, handy hints, and interesting snippets help visitors make the most of their time in New York.

Feature Boxes

Notable topics are highlighted in these special boxes.

Key Facts Box

This box gives details of the distance covered on the tour, plus an estimate of how long it should take. It also states where the tour starts and finishes, and gives key travel information such as which days are best to do the tour or handy transport tips.

Route Map

Detailed cartography with the walk or tour clearly plotted with numbered dots. For more detailed mapping, see the pull-out map slotted inside the back cover.

Footers

The footers on the left-hand pages give the itinerary name, plus, where relevant, a map reference; those on the right-hand pages cite the main attraction on the double page.

Food and Drink

Recommendations of where to stop for refreshment are given in these boxes. The numbers prior to each café/restaurant name link to references in the main text. Places recommended en route are also plotted on the maps.

The **$** signs at the end of each entry reflect the approximate cost of a three-course meal for one. These should be seen as a guide only. Price ranges, which are also quoted on the inside back flap for easy reference, are as follows:

$$$$ over $70
$$$ $50–70
$$ $25–50
$ under $25

SKYSCRAPER SPOTTING

Explore the vertical city, including New York's first skyscraper, the Flatiron (walk 11), the Art Deco-era Chrysler (walk 4), and Empire State (walk 1), modern, eco-friendly Hearst Tower (walk 8), and high-rise Lower Manhattan (walk 15).

RECOMMENDED TOURS FOR...

FOODIES

For fresh produce try Union Square Greenmarket (walk 11) or Chelsea Market (walk 11), while Dean & Deluca (walk 13) and Katz's Delicatessen (walk 14) are packed with gourmet goodies.

ART ENTHUSIASTS

There's more art than can be seen in a lifetime: from the big five – the Met (tour 6), MoMA (tour 3), Whitney, Guggenheim, and Frick (walk 7) – to Chelsea's gallery scene (walk 11).

SPECTACULAR VIEWS

Take in glorious views from the Empire State Building (walk 1), Top of the Rock at Rockefeller Center (walk 1), Brooklyn Bridge (walk 17), Statue of Liberty (tour 16), or Staten Island Ferry (tour 16).

PARKS AND GARDENS

Central Park (walk 5) is a masterpiece of lands architecture, but don't overlook the New York Botanical Garden (walk 18) in the Bronx or th Brooklyn Botanic Garden (walk 17).

SHOPPERS

Go on a shopping spree at Fifth Avenue department stores (walk 1); check out boutiques in Soho (walk 13), NoLita (walk 14), and the Meatpacking District (walk 12); and browse 18 miles of books at the Strand Book Store (walk 12).

MOVIE BUFFS' NEW YORK

King Kong clambered up the Empire State Building (walk 1); Holly Golightly breakfasted at Tiffany's (walk 1); Clark Kent reported in the News Building (walk 4); Travis Bickle wandered Times Square (walk 2); and the Corleones caused big trouble in Little Italy (walk 14).

NIGHTLIFE

Check out the alt-rock scene on the Lower East Side (walk 14); catch a set at a Greenwich Village jazz club (walk 12) or Harlem's Apollo (walk 9); or dance all night at a Meatpacking District hotspot (walk 12).

CHILDREN

Visit dinosaurs at the American Museum of Natural History (walk 8) or penguins at Central Park Zoo (walk 5), then shop for toys at FAO Schwarz (walk 1).

THE PERFORMING ARTS

Take in a Broadway show on the Great White Way (walk 2); the symphony, opera, or ballet at Lincoln Center (walk 8); an off-Broadway romp in the East Village (walk 14); or a free performance of Shakespeare in the Park (walk 5).

OVERVIEW

An overview of New York's geography, character, and culture, plus illuminating background information on food and drink, shopping, and history.

CITY INTRODUCTION

Most of the 45 million visitors who come to the Big Apple each year arrive with skyscraper-high expectations. Jaw-dropping architecture, world-class cultural attractions, a hugely vibrant creative scene, and fabulous shops and restaurants – all in a city that never stands still – are not likely to disappoint.

What's in a Name?
It remains open to debate how New York got its 'Big Apple' tag. Some say that the nickname came from a 1920s newspaper column about horse racing called 'Around the Big Apple.' Others say it was used by jazz players to indicate getting to the top of their profession, or reaching 'the Big Apple.'

In his writings on the city, *Here is New York*, the children's author, critic, and Pulitzer Prize-winner E.B. White wrote, 'New York is nothing like Paris; it is nothing like London; and it is not Spokane multiplied by sixty, or Detroit multiplied by four. It is by all odds the loftiest of cities. It even managed to reach the highest point in the sky at the lowest moment of the Depression.'

Since its purchase by the Dutch in 1626, through its growth as a maritime hub, to its contemporary position as the cultural and financial center of the United States, New York his risen to become a crossroads of the world and a place where the air tingles with the promise that everything is possible.

Statistics

The statistics are quite something: 6,400 miles (10,300km) of streets, 578 miles (930km) of waterfront, 18,000 restaurants, around 13,000 taxis, over 6,000 city buses, 150 museums, and 400 art galleries, more than 240 theaters, and 28,000 acres (11,330 hectares) of parks. Whatever you're after, from world-class museums on the Upper East Side to cutting-edge couture in the Meatpacking District, you'll find it here. If you stay in a sky-high hotel far above the teeming streets, or stroll in Central Park, or walk out onto the terrace overlooking the Hudson River at the Cloisters, you may even be able to find that city-center rarity: peace and quiet.

Right: a yellow taxi cab pulls out into Times Square.

THE BOROUGHS

New York City covers a surface area of 321.8 sq miles (833 sq km), and is divided into five boroughs: Manhattan, Brooklyn, Queens, the Bronx, and Staten Island. Manhattan, the smallest borough, has a surface area of just over 22 sq miles (57 sq km), but is the most densely populated part of the city.

NEW YORKERS

Population and Melting Pot

According to the US Census Bureau, New York City has a population of 8 million. Of that figure, approximately 1.5 million people reside in Manhattan, 2.4 million in Brooklyn, 2.2 million in Queens, 1.3 million in the Bronx, and around 440,000 in Staten Island.

Although there are other cities in the United States with a high percentage of foreign-born residents, none can match the range or diversity of the ethnic communities of New York. Here, around 35 percent of inhabitants are of European descent, 24.5 percent are African-American or African-Caribbean, 27 percent are Hispanic, and 9.8 percent are Asian. A former mayor David Dinkins once described the city as a 'gorgeous mosaic.'

The Classic New Yorker

New Yorkers are stereotypically portrayed as being as relentlessly energetic as their home town is fast-paced. Frenetic or not (recent polls have shown that New York is not quite as super-speedy as its reputation might suggest – a 2007 survey of urban walking speeds put New Yorkers in only eighth place, after Singapore and Copenhagen), this energy is perhaps what gives New Yorkers their edge and makes them so sure that Manhattan is the center of the universe. Increasing numbers are choosing to retire in the city, lured by the ease of getting around and the many attractions.

Resilience is also a key attribute. The reaction of most city inhabitants to the attacks of September 11, 2001, when terrorists crashed two hijacked jets into the towering World Trade Center, was to respond with characteristic resolve to recover and rebuild.

Above from far left: Manhattan from Brooklyn Bridge; Beaux Arts grandeur at Grand Central Terminal; after hours in the city that never sleeps; the Chrysler Building.

Below: New Yorker, New York.

Above from left:
hanging out in the West Village; the Guggenheim Museum on Fifth Avenue; spinning turntables in a Tribeca bar; Lower Manhattan skyline.

CLIMATE

New York is blessed with sunshine year-round, but it has four distinct seasons. Summers can be steamy, with temperatures as high as 96°F (36°C), and winter days may dip as low as 10°F (-12°C). Happily, extreme heat or cold spells are usually brief; typical summer day temperatures are around 85°F (29°C) and winters in the 30–45°F (-1–7°C) range. Snowfalls are generally light, though every few years a major storm blankets the city, which thrills cross-country skiers, who head for Central Park. April brings showers, but May and June can be delightful, and the bright fall weather in September and October makes this the ideal time to visit. Spring and fall days average 60–75°F (15–24°C).

WATERWAYS

New York lies at the mouth of the Hudson River, which borders Manhattan's West Side. On the other side, the East River, separating Manhattan from Brooklyn and Queens, is a narrow strip of water linking Long Island Sound and Upper New York Bay. The southern portions of Brooklyn and Queens have sandy shores on the Atlantic Ocean. It is estimated that it takes an average of seven hours and 15 minutes to swim around Manhattan (not recommended).

WALKERS' CITY

Unlike many cities in the United States, New York is a great place for walkers, helped by the fact that for the most part it is organized on a straightforward grid plan – numbered streets (north–south) and avenues (east–west). Pay little heed to the fancied-up Avenue of the Americas tag for good old Sixth Avenue, but watch out for the crazy-quilt pattern below 14th Street.

The West Village has streets unique to its neighborhood, many running at odd angles, which makes navigating this area a fun challenge even for long-time New Yorkers. Things really change south of Houston Street, where the numbered streets end altogether. Keep in mind that Fifth Avenue and, to the north, Central Park, mark the division between east and west.

Staying Safe

Some people fear walking around New York because of supposed pickpockets or would-be attackers, but in fact the city has had a sharp decline in the rate of crime in recent years, and has been named one of America's safest large cities. Such crime that does occur tends to be as random in nature as absolutely anywhere else in the world, and, as elsewhere, ostentatious displays of jewelry or wealth tend to invite unwanted attention.

Since New York is generally a lively place at all hours, there are only a few locations you should avoid. Most streets are consistently populated – although Midtown and southern Manhattan business areas are more deserted in the evenings, when the East and West Villages and Theatre District are hopping. Central Park,

Yellow Taxis
New York taxis date from 1907, when John Hertz founded the Yellow Cab Company. He chose this color after reading a study that said that yellow was the easiest to spot.

Battery Park, and Harlem are best avoided after dark.

SUBWAYS, BUSES, TAXIS

In addition to the city being so straightforward to navigate on foot, it also has excellent subway and bus systems. Ask for free maps at subway stations and on buses. Despite reports to the contrary, subways are considered fairly clean and safe – although it's still best to avoid traveling on your own after 11pm. The subway is usually the fastest way of getting around, especially for long distances, although walking can be quicker if you're only traveling a few blocks.

Buses are useful and, while slow during rush hours, may seem less intimidating than navigating the subway. They are also a cheap way to see the sights. Each bus has a digital destination sign, and maps are posted at every stop.

Those iconic yellow taxis easy to become dependent on – unlike many cities, where you have to arrange for taxis in advance, in New York they just seem to appear (except when it's raining) and can be hailed anywhere you spot the light signifying the cab is available. Fares can mount up fast. If you're trying to get somewhere at rush hour, it can be a long, frustrating, and expensive ride, and it's probably a better idea to catch the subway.

An Exceptional City

By the end of their first trip to New York, most visitors are hooked.

Nothing is quite as exhilarating as walking between the skyscrapers of Midtown for the first time, or seeing the iconic Statue of Liberty looming over you from the ferry dock. Or even just strolling through Central Park on a sunny day or a blustery winter afternoon. Remember to walk purposefully and you'll fit right in. You'll soon discover why New Yorkers have a right to feel that there's no place quite like their home.

Long Island Beaches
Although New York lies on the coast, the beaches accessible by public transportation tend to be crowded, especially on hot summer weekends. The nicest are half a day's trip away from Manhattan, on Long Island.

Urban Woodland

When Henry Hudson sailed up the river that bears his name, his first mate, Robert Juett, wrote: 'We found a land full of great tall oaks, with grass and flowers, as pleasant as ever has been seen.' New York still has over 28,000 acres (11,300 hectares) of parks, of which 10,000 acres (4,000 hectares) are wooded. Peregrine falcons nest on Midtown skyscraper ledges, and coyotes occasionally prowl from Westchester County down into the Bronx. Frederick Law Olmsted, the architect who laid out Central Park, wrote that, 'the contemplation of natural scenes... is favorable to the health and vigor of men.'

FOOD AND DRINK

Visitors will quickly discover why New Yorkers are passionate about food. The city boasts an amazing variety of delicious choices, haute cuisine to street carts, with prices to match.

Cookery Classes
The nation's largest cooking school, the Institute of Culinary Education, is on 23rd Street between Sixth and Seventh avenues. It offers several half-day classes most days. For information, see www.iceculinary.com.

Below: alfresco lunch on a sunny day.

New York has always had a reputation as a culinary melting pot. From Jewish delicatessens to Mexican taco joints to the United Nations Delegates' Dining Room *(see p.41)*, people can enjoy a staggering range of food at every price range. They can order a $2 hot dog at Gray's Papaya *(see p.117)* or a $32 hamburger at DB Bistro Moderne *(see p.29)*. Diners are a New York institution found in almost every neighborhood, serving from breakfast through dinner with a wide variety of choices from snacks, sandwiches, and salads to full meals, all at moderate prices. The city's top-drawer restaurants take pride in serving the very best of French cuisine.

FASHIONS IN FOOD

Fashions are vital in New York, and the contemporary fashion is for famous-name kitchens fronted by celebrity chefs, both homegrown and from as far afield as London, Paris, and Italy. Current stars include Jean-Georges Vongerichten, Alain Ducasse, and Daniel Boulud.

Another current fashion is to preface food styles by the words 'haute' and 'real,' stressing quality and authenticity. 'Haute Italian' describes Italian cuisine at its most elaborate, for example. Menus that change with the seasons, stressing foods fresh from local farms, are points of pride for many restaurants, as are organically grown vegetables and preservative-free meats and poultry.

Special Diets

While 'vegetarian' has graduated from a regular option to a mainstay, with vegan choices increasingly available, the extreme theme is continued with diets containing the prefix 'free' ('dairy-

free' or 'wheat-free,' for example). These terms are sprinkled over all but the least fashionable menus in New York, making it possible for everyone to find suitable food, whatever their dietary requirements.

TRENDS BY AREA

Midtown

Some of the world's finest and most expensive restaurants – the Four Seasons *(see p.116)*, Le Bernardin, and Alain Ducasse's Adour at the St Regis to name but a few – are located in Midtown. Many Manhattan mainstays are here too, with the longevity prize going to the fabulous nonagenarian Oyster Bar *(see p.43)* at Grand Central Terminal.

For Midtown dining, it pays to do your homework. While spontaneity is fun farther Downtown, in Midtown it's best to make reservations, especially to dine before or after the theater.

Restaurants here, especially the more expensive ones, often have formal dress codes. Men are suited (or at least jacketed) and women go groomed for a glamorous night on the town. Many Midtown restaurants are closed Sundays, and for lunch on Saturdays, as their corporate customers have gone.

Meatpacking District, Chelsea, Soho, and Tribeca

The Meatpacking District is good for both dining and posing, even if the patrons are often wafer-thin models who look as if they never eat. Chelsea

Market *(see p.74)*, at Ninth Avenue and 15th Street, is heaven for food fetishists – a dozen or so bakeries, meat markets, kitchen suppliers, and other stores of a gastronomic bent, along with trendy dining places.

Once Soho gained recognition as an artistic center, people began streaming here in search of 'the scene.' The restaurant tariffs reflect Soho's now-dominant chicness, but there's no need to go hungry, or to pay through the nose. You can shell out $35+ for a steak at Balthazar *(see p.85)*, but you can also eat for plenty less at Fanelli Cafe *(see p.83)*.

In bordering Tribeca, the star element plays a big part, this time in the shape of actor Robert De Niro. Now one of Tribeca's most famous diners, he moved here in 1976, and began investing in restaurants such as Nobu *(see p.121)*, and the Tribeca Grill *(see p.85)*. He promoted his 'hood as a cool area in which to hang out, and it still is.

East Village and Lower East Side

While once there was little reason to venture into these neighborhoods, and certainly not at night, they now come alive when the sun goes down, and, for many New Yorkers, the best two reasons to visit the Lower East Side and East Village are to drink and to dine.

The once-mean streets of the Lower East Side, an enclave of immigration in previous centuries, are now very much the domain of hipsters. To witness this renaissance, check out the restaurants around Ludlow and

Above from far left: a New York diner; the $32 burger at DB Bistro Moderne *(see p.29)*; taking a break at Dean & Deluca *(see p.84)*; a chef at work in an open kitchen.

Best to Reserve Reservations are essential. Unless you plan to eat at a diner or cafeteria, be sure to call ahead. If you plan on going to a new venue that everybody's raving about, call days, if not weeks, in advance. And even if you have 'resos,' don't be surprised if you still have to wait a while to be seated. The only surefire way of beating the crowds is to eat at off-hours.

Above from left:
cocktails on the
Lower East Side;
waterside dining in
Lower Manhattan.

Clinton streets. Even the once-lowly Bowery is becoming a restaurant mecca. For a taste of the area's heritage, however, visit Katz's Delicatessen *(see p.88)* or seek out the colorful, inexpensive Indian restaurants along Sixth Street between Second and First avenues, known collectively as Curry Row.

For a look at the East Village scene, check out hip bars and restaurants along avenues A and B, although expect to feel old if you're over 40, unfashionable if you're wearing a color other than black, and out of sync if you show up before 10 o'clock.

The Bagel Debate

The fastest way to start an argument among New Yorkers is to ask them where to find the best bagels in town. The rings of bread dough, first boiled then baked, were introduced to New York in the 1880s by East European Jews and have since become a local staple. They come in any number of varieties – sesame, poppy, onion, raisin, among others – and are traditionally eaten with a *schmear* of cream cheese and perhaps a slice of lox (smoked salmon) and red onion. Uptown favorites include H&H Bagel (2239 Broadway at 80th Street), Lenny's Bagels (2601 Broadway at 98th Street), and Tal Bagel (333 East 86th Street near Second Avenue). In Midtown, look for Ess-a-Bagel (831 Third Avenue at

50th Street) and Pick a Bagel on Third (297 Third Avenue at 22nd Street). Downtown is longtime favorite Kossar's (367 Grand Street near Essex Street), which specializes in 'bialys,' a close cousin to the bagel but without the hole.

Upper West Side

This part of town, home to the Lincoln Center and the focal point of the New York Jewish community, is good for understated neighborhood dining. Columbus Circle and the Lincoln Center area have fine-dining choices, long topped by Jean-Georges *(see p.117)*. The arrival of the Time Warner Center upped the culinary sweepstakes (with price tags) even higher, with Michael Lomonaco's highly regarded Porter House New York, Thomas Keller's 'edible art' at Per Se (expect a tab of $275!), and the always-booked Masa, current holder of the highest price tag of any Manhattan dining experience. Keller's Bouchon Bakery offers light meals and decadent desserts with a far less stratospheric tab.

Upper East Side

With sky-high real-estate prices and stores to match, the upscale Upper East Side is where ladies of leisure like to lunch. You can dine very well indeed in this part of town, and the neighborhood demographics supply the sort of crowd that appreciates upmarket dining. Many of the neighborhood's best restaurants are old standbys that seem tailor-made for special occasions, or to wine and dine a client or a visiting in-law. The neighborhood has attracted chefs such as Daniel Boulud and Philippe Bertineau, in search of customers with refined taste buds and big dining budgets.

For the most part, the best restaurants are concentrated in the western part of the neighborhood, on leafy streets lined with palatial townhouses

and white-glove apartment houses. In general, the farther east you go, the younger the restaurant crowd bcomes – Second Avenue, especially, is noted for its noisy bars and eateries catering to restless singles on the prowl.

BRUNCH

Weekends are when New Yorkers stroll instead of sprint. On Saturday and Sunday mornings, restaurants are filled with Manhattanites enjoying a slow start to the day, eating brunch in the company of a friend, with a partner or spouse, or alone with the newspaper or a book. Sunday brunch in particular is a local tradition.

Most restaurants offer a set-price brunch menu, but there are some stand-out choices. In the heart of Central Park on the edge of a pond dotted with colorful rowboats, the Boathouse *(see p.46)* wins the prize for charm. The menu is good, too; try the smoked salmon frittata, French toast or steak and eggs. For the best French-inspired brunch, head for Balthazar *(see p.85)* in Soho, and dip your croissant into a gigantic cup of the house hot chocolate. For bohemian appeal, head out to Brooklyn, which excels at laidback weekends.

Gourmet Food
Vital to New York's food culture are gourmet shops, delicatessens, and bakeries. At the high end are Zabar's, Dean & Deluca, and Barney Greengrass, which carry premium meats, fish, cheeses, baked goods, and prepared foods. More modest in size (but not quality) are mom-and-pop ethnic stores: traditional Italian and Jewish delicatessens, bagel shops, pastry shops, and Asian markets.

Left: on Saturday and Sunday it's time for brunch.

SHOPPING

There are few more exciting places to shop than this Cornucopia-on-the-Hudson, with its boutiques, department stores, and discount outlets all jostling for a piece of the sales action.

Opening Times
Each shopping area tends to have slightly different opening times – the general rule is that Downtown stores open and close an hour or two later than Uptown. Most department stores and many other shops open Mon–Sat 10am–6pm, with evening hours on Thur. Some stay open until 8pm or 9pm on a regular basis and are also open on Sun.

When the city's wealthy began migrating from Lower Manhattan to the north, New York stores followed suit. From the 1860s to around 1920, shopping was concentrated in what is now the Ladies Mile Historic District. The heart was roughly from 14th to 24th streets along Sixth Avenue. The opening of the Sixth Avenue elevated line in 1878 provided access for shoppers from all over the city. But as the better residential areas continued moving north in the early 1900s, the stores again followed, opening quarters in Midtown, where the larger stores remain today. Shopping, however, is not limited to any one area. Every neighborhood has its share of lures, suited to the tastes and budgets of its residents. A general rule of thumb is that the most elegant boutiques are Uptown, the big department stores are in Midtown, and the funkier boutiques are Downtown. Wherever you roam in New York, shopping is part of the fun.

Below: the Lower East Side is good for vintage fashion.

DEPARTMENT STORES

New York is still known for its department stores, selling everything from dishes to designer fashions. Macy's bills itself as 'the world's largest department store' *(see p.35)*. Lord & Taylor, a few blocks north, and Bloomingdales at 1003 Third Avenue at 60th Street (entrances also on Lexington Avenue), cater to a slightly more upscale market. A notch higher still are Saks Fifth Avenue *(see p.31)* and Bergdorf Goodman *(see p.31)*, both luxury stores selling mostly clothes and accessories. Barney's at 660 Madison Avenue and 61st Street is the *ne plus ultra* for pricey cutting-edge fashions.

WHAT TO BUY

Fashion
Look to 57th Street between 5th and Madison avenues and Madison Avenue above 60th Street for elegant, expensive boutiques, to Soho for high-end fashion, to Fifth Avenue for reliable labels, and to NoLita and the Lower East Side for cutting-edge designs and valuable vintage. The Meatpacking District is home to many high-profile designers *(see p.81)*. For high fashion at low prices, head for Century 21 Department Store (22 Cortland Street between

Church Street and Broadway in Lower Manhattan), where designer labels can be had at substantial discounts. Daffy's is another discount chain with several locations around town.

Art and Antiques

The city has hundreds of art galleries, from major auction houses like Sotheby's to the avant-garde galleries in Chelsea *(see p.74)*. Traditional galleries tend to be found on East 57th Street and on the upper East Side. Only a few galleries remain in Soho.

A good neighborhood for antiques is 10th and 12th streets between University Place and Broadway. Manhattan Art & Antiques Center (1050 Second Avenue at 56th Street) has dozens of dealers under one roof, as does the Chelsea Antiques Building (110 West 25th Street between Sixth and Seventh avenues). ABC Carpet & Home (888 Broadway at 19th Street) has several floors of unique furniture, accessories, and carpets from all over the world.

For flea-market finds, check the weekend offerings at Hell's Kitchen Flea Market (West 39th Street between Ninth and Tenth avenues), Antiques Garage (112 West 25th Street between Sixth and Seventh avenues), and the Green Flea Market (Columbus Avenue between 76th and 77th streets, *see p.63*).

Books

Barnes & Noble dominates the market with its many superstores, and Borders also has a presence in the city. Stores of both usually have cafés and book-readings. Greenwich Village is a great place to shop for books and records; for secondhand and antiquarian titles pay a visit to the Strand Book Store *(see p.78)*, which claims to have 2 million volumes in stock. (There's a second branch at 95 Fulton Street.) Some unusual specialty shops include the Drama Book Shop (250 West 40th Street between Seventh and Eighth avenues), Books of Wonder for children (16 West 18th Street between Fifth and Sixth avenues), Mysterious Bookshop for mysteries (58 Warren Street between West Broadway and Church Street), and Kitchen Arts & Letters for chefs (1435 Lexington Avenue between 93rd and 94th streets).

Electronics

One of the best places to buy cameras and photographic equipment is bustling B&H Photo-Video at 420 Ninth Avenue at 34th Street (tel: 212-444-6615). Opening hours vary; call ahead.

Another good bet is J&R Music World at 23 Park Row, across from City Hall. And if you want to indulge in the latest iPod, visit the city's fabulous flagship Apple Store on Fifth Avenue; there's also a store on 103 Prince Street at Mercer Street in Soho and on Broadway at 67th Street.

Some smaller places don't offer warranties on electronic goods, so check before you buy.

GIFTS

Museum shops are reliable sources for unusual gifts, and don't forget the Public Library gift shop.

Above from far left: Macy's – 'the world's largest department store'; caps at a street market; Strand Book Store – a New York institution; toy shops include FAO Schwarz *(see p.30)*.

The Sales
Sales are held after the Christmas holidays and in mid-July. Department stores tend to offer the best markdowns. Holiday weekends – Fourth of July etc. – are also prime sale times. Barney's legendary warehouse sale in mid-August draws big crowds. For manufacturers' sample sales, check topbutton.com.

ENTERTAINMENT

From the bright lights of Broadway to the stage of the Metropolitan Opera, symphony at Carnegie Hall to jazz or ballet at Lincoln Center, New York is America's Entertainment Capital, with an unending parade of world-class attractions.

When You Need a Laugh…
New York has many top comedy clubs. Two of the best are Caroline's on Broadway (1626 Broadway between 49th and 50th streets; tel: 212-757-4100; www.caronines.com) and Comix (363 West 14th Street between Eighth and Ninth avenues; tel: 212-524-2500; www.comixny.com).

Mention New York and most visitors think Broadway, with good reason. New York has been a theater mecca since the proliferation of lights in the early 1900s caused the street to become known as the 'Great White Way.' Almost 12 million patrons attend a Broadway show in an average year.

The city has been equally important in music. The Metropolitan Opera, founded in 1880, is world-renowned, and New York has been a popular music center since the days of Tin Pan Alley in the early 1900s. The heritage continues at Lincoln Center *(see p.64 and 123)*, one of the largest performing arts centers in the world, home to twelve resident organizations including opera, ballet, symphony, chamber music, jazz, theater, and film. New York clubs, always on the cutting edge, have been influential in the development of genres from swing to jazz, rock to rap.

THEATER

Besides the dozens of theaters on and around Broadway, New York has several non-profit repertory companies, performing both new works and revivals; many of these go on to take their shows to Broadway *(see p.122)*. The city also boasts well over 100 smaller theaters with 100 to 500 seats known as 'off-Broadway,' and countless interesting venues with fewer than 100 seats known as 'off-off Broadway.' Pioneering off-Broadway companies such as Playwrights Horizons have nurtured major new works, including *Driving Miss Daisy* and Sondheim's *Sunday in the Park with George*. See listings for all shows at www.off-Broadway.com.

For shows offering ticket discounts, see www.theatermania.com or www.playbill.com. The TKTS booth *(see p.33)* at 46th Street and Broadway has half-price tickets to same-day productions that are not sold out.

DANCE

The New York City Ballet, one of America's premier companies, has spring and winter seasons in the David H. Koch Theater at Lincoln Center *(see p.64)*. Its delightful Christmas season production of *The Nutcracker* is a well-loved tradition. Another major troupe, the American Ballet Theater, visits for a spring season at the Metropolitan Opera House and a fall season at varying

venues. New York City Center *(see p.123)* also hosts important dance groups, both modern and traditional, including Alvin Ailey and Paul Taylor, and the Joyce Theater is a year-round stage for modern dance troupes from around the world.

MUSIC

At Lincoln Center, Avery Fisher Hall is the home stage for the New York Philharmonic while Alice Tully Hall features chamber groups. Avery Fisher also hosts the annual summer Mostly Mozart Festival. The Metropolitan Opera season runs from October through April, the more affordable New York City Opera performs late October through November and March–April at the David H. Koch Theater. The Juilliard School of Music offers many free concerts by its talented faculty and students.

Jazz at Lincoln Center has expansive separate quarters at the Time Warner Center *(see p.65)* that include Dizzy's Club Coca-Cola *(see p.65)*. Other well-known jazz clubs include the Blue Note and Village Vanguard *(see p.77)*. Additionally, Harlem has legendary jazz clubs such as the Lenox Lounge *(see p.67)*. For rock and other music of the day, the Beacon Theater and the Bowery Ballroom *(see p.122)* are popular spots.

FILM/MOVIES

Film buffs will find a rich menu in New York, beginning with the Walter Reade Theater (www.filmlinc.com), home to the Film Society of Lincoln Center and the New York Film Festival from late September through mid-October. Other theaters showing independent and art films include Lincoln Plaza Cinema, the Landmark Sunshine Cinema, the Angelika, Film Center, the IFC Center, Film Forum, and the theater of the Museum of Modern Art *(see p.37)*. The Tribeca Film Festival begun by Robert De Niro takes place in late April–early May.

NIGHTLIFE

The city's myriad bars and clubs offer every ambience from refined to raucous, and something for every age and taste. The late night dance club scene frequented by young New Yorkers tends to be found Downtown, in the Meat Packing District or in Hell's Kitchen, on the far west side in the 40s. Hot clubs are often hidden in unexpected places like warehouses or lofts.

Above from far left
Jazz musician Wynton Marsalis performs at Lincoln Center; catch a major musical on Broadway; New York's dance clubs are legendary; a ballet dancer from *The Nutcracker* signs autographs.

Half-Price Tickets
For same-day bargains on Broadway, try the TKTS booth *(see left)*, and for Lincoln Center, the David Rubenstein Atrium.

Sports Headliners

Sports are always in season in New York, and watching a thrilling game is fun for visitors and residents alike. The city offers major teams in every arena: Yankee and Mets baseball April through September, Knicks basketball October through April, Giants and Jets football September through early January, Rangers hockey October through April. and Red Bulls soccer March through October. The US Open Tennis Championship in late August is a world-class Grand Slam event. For current schedules, see www.nyc.go (go to 'what to do,' 'sports').

HISTORY: KEY DATES

*From a small Dutch trading post to the Crossroads of the World, the rise of
New York has been accompanied by civil war, mass immigration, riots and
recession, terrorism, and triumph.*

NEW AMSTERDAM

1524	Giovanni da Varrazzano is the first European to step onto the island known to the local Algonquin Indians as Mannahatta.
1624	The Dutch West India Company establishes a settlement (New Amsterdam) on the southern tip of Mannahatta (now Battery Park).
1664	War between England and Holland. New Amsterdam surrenders and is renamed New York after Charles II's brother, James, Duke of York.

INDEPENDENCE TO CIVIL WAR

1776	The Revolutionary War begins; the colonies declare independence. British troops occupy New York until 1783.
1789–90	New York is capital of the new United States of America.
1790	The first official census: New York has a population of 33,000.
1811	The decision is made to lay out the city's streets in a grid pattern.
1830	Irish and German immigrants begin arriving in great numbers.
1835	Part of Manhattan is ravaged by the 'Great Fire.'
1848–9	Political refugees arrive after failure of the German Revolution.
1858	Calvert Vaux and Frederick Law Olmsted submit plans for Central Park.
1861–5	American Civil War. New York is on the winning, Yankee side.

LATE 19TH CENTURY

1865	Italians, Jews, and Chinese begin arriving in large numbers.
1869	The Museum of Natural History opens.
1880	The Metropolitan Museum of Art opens.
1883	The Brooklyn Bridge opens. The Metropolitan Opera stages its debut performance.
1886	The Statue of Liberty, a gift from France, is unveiled.
1892	Ellis Island becomes the entry point for immigrants. More than 12 million immigrants pass through the facility before it is closed in 1954.
1898	New York's five boroughs unite under one municipal government.

Peter Stuyvesant,
director general of
New Amsterdam
(1647–64), erected a
barricade against the
Indians and British
on the site of what is
now Wall Street.

20TH CENTURY

1902	Completion of Flatiron Building, briefly the world's tallest building.
1904	A subway system is established.
1913	Erection of the world's tallest skyscraper, the Woolworth Building, begins. It is superseded in 1930 by the Chrysler Building.
1917–18	US intervenes in World War I.
1929	Wall Street Crash and start of the Great Depression.
1931	Empire State Building opens, taking the title of world's tallest building.
1933–45	Europeans take refuge in New York from Nazi persecution.
1941	US enters World War II.
1946	United Nations begins meeting in New York.
1959	Guggenheim Museum opens. Work begins on the Lincoln Center.
1970	The city suffers from economic decline that continues until *c.*1976.
1973	The 110-story World Trade Center opens, the world's tallest building at the time.
1975	The city avoids bankruptcy via a loan from the Federal government.
1986	Battery Park City opens.
1987	'Black Monday' on Wall Street; shares suffer a sudden 30 percent drop in value. A bomb explodes below the World Trade Center.
1990	David Dinkins becomes the city's first African-American mayor.
1993	Rudolph Giuliani voted in as mayor and gets 'tough on crime.'

21ST CENTURY

2000	Crowds flock to revitalized Times Square to see in the millennium.
2001	Terrorists crash two hijacked planes into the Twin Towers of the World Trade Center. The buildings collapse, killing close to 3,000 people. Michael Bloomberg is elected mayor.
2003	Power blackout plunges New York into darkness. FBI survey finds New York safest large city in the US.
2004	Museum of Modern Art reopens in Manhattan after major expansion.
2006	Work begins on the *Reflecting Absence* memorial at Ground Zero.
2008	Democratic Senator Barack Obama elected the first black president of the United States. Wall Street experiences the worst financial crisis since the Great Depression.
2009	Michael Bloomberg elected for an unprecedented third term as mayor. New baseball stadiums open for the Yankees and the Mets. High Line Park opens to the public.
2010	Lincoln Center renovation completed. Despite continuing recession, tourism numbers on course for a record 47.5 million visitors.

WALKS AND TOURS

1

FIFTH AVENUE

Few streets evoke the essence of the city as powerfully as Fifth Avenue, with its iconic Empire State Building, glorious Rockefeller Center, stylish shopping, and elegant St Patrick's Cathedral.

DISTANCE 1½ miles (2.5km)
TIME A half-day
START Empire State Building
END Grand Army Plaza
POINTS TO NOTE

Try to get to the Empire State Building as early as possible to avoid long lines. Or come back at dusk for sunset and a spectacular view of Manhattan at night. The Top of the Rock offers an alternative view of the city skyline with shorter lines.

Once the playground of Gotham's wealthiest families, today Fifth Avenue is most people's image of Manhattan. Here are the city's most famous skyscraper, best views, landmark building, and signature stores.

EMPIRE STATE BUILDING

Rising like a rocket above 34th Street and Fifth Avenue is the **Empire State Building** ❶ (tel: 212-736-3100; www. esbnyc.com; observatory daily 8am–2am, last ascent at 1.15am; charge). When it opened in 1931, this Art Deco landmark was the tallest building in the world; today, it ranks behind skyscrapers in Taipei, Kuala Lumpur, and Chicago, among others. Still, the view from the 86th-floor Observatory is incomparable: on a clear day you can see as far as 80 miles (128km) away.

This is the place where a forlorn Cary Grant waited for Deborah Kerr in *An Affair to Remember* (1957), where Tom Hanks hooked up with Meg Ryan in *Sleepless in Seattle* (1993), and where Fay Wray had a rendezvous with a tall, dark leading man of a more brutish disposition in *King Kong* (1933).

Ticket Options

Lines at the security checkpoint, ticket booth, and elevator can be horrendous, but you can save time by buying tickets online. Although you still have to pass through security and wait for an elevator, you won't need to wait hours to get a ticket. If you have money to burn, you could buy an 'Express Pass Ticket,' entitling the holder to move to the front of all lines. For an additional fee, you can also purchase 102nd-floor **Observatory** tickets, which are sold only at the ticket office on the second floor.

New York Skyride

The **New York Skyride** is a simulated flight around the city narrated by actor Kevin Bacon. Unless you're traveling with children, you may wish to skip this, as a virtual experience of the skyline seems slightly redundant when the real

thing is only an elevator away. The only advantage of a Skyride ticket is that it gives you a shortcut to the Observatory.

Once you're back down on the ground, if you're feeling hungry, there are numerous places nearby. For carnivorous cravings try **Keen's Steakhouse**, see ⑪①, two blocks north on West 36th Street.

NEW YORK PUBLIC LIBRARY

Continue north on legendary Fifth Avenue. Although the magnificent townhouses once owned here by such eminent dynasties as the Astors and Vanderbilts have been replaced by less glamorous discount shops and computer stores, the old grandeur can still be found at the elegant Beaux Arts **New York Public Library** ❷ (tel: 212-930-0830; www.nypl.org; Mon–Sat 10am–6pm, Tue–Wed until 9pm; free access and daily tours) at 42nd Street.

With its Corinthian columns and white Vermont marble, its palatial staircases, and famous sculpted lions *(see margin, right)* standing guard out front, the 1911 building is a landmark of its kind, ranking with such select

Food and Drink 🍴

① KEEN'S STEAKHOUSE
72 West 36th Street (near Sixth Avenue); tel: 212-947-3636; Mon–Fri L and D, Sat–Sun D; $$$
In business since 1885, this classic American steakhouse serves up thick slabs of beef and mutton.

Above from far left: inside the lobby of the Empire State Building; Paul Manship's statue *Prometheus Bringing Fire to the World*, at Rockefeller Plaza; bibliophilic sentiment at the New York Public Library; view of the Empire State Building from the Top of the Rock *(see p.30).*

Library Lions
The grand stone lions at the entrance to the New York Public Library were sculpted by Edward Clark Potter and originally named Astor and Lenox after the library's benefactors. Nowadays, they are better known as Patience and Fortitude, nicknames bestowed upon them by Depression-era Mayor Fiorello LaGuardia.

French Style

Step into the opulent lobby of the Fred R. French building on Fifth Avenue at 45th Street to see a prime example of a flamboyant period in New York architecture. Built in 1927 for a real-estate tycoon, it was designed to impress, with a vaulted polychrome ceiling and polished bronze doors.

worthies as the Morgan Library *(see box, below)*, and Grand Central Terminal *(see p.43)*. The building's architects were John Merven Carrère and Thomas Hastings, Paris-trained partners who triumphed in a design competition.

Reading Room

Not to be missed is the majestic third-floor Main Reading Room, brilliantly renovated in 1998 at a cost of $15 million. Its vast perimeter is lined with reference works surrounding lamp-lit desks, at which readers digest books summoned with 'call slips' from the library's vast hidden recesses. Free

tours are offered daily from Astor Hall at the library's entrance.

Among the books, maps, manuscripts, periodicals, photographs, and varied items numbering in the millions in this building are the first Gutenberg Bible brought to America, Christopher Columbus's 1493 account of his momentous voyage, George Washington's own handwritten *Farewell Address*, and Thomas Jefferson's early draft of the *Declaration of Independence*.

Head two blocks north to West 44th Street for a liquid lunch at the **Algonquin Hotel**, see ⑪③, or posh bistro fare at **DB Bistro Moderne**, see ⑪④.

The Morgan Library & Museum

Billionaire J.P. Morgan (1837–1913), known for his consolidation of railroad and steel empires, was an expert collector with taste and wealth, both well displayed at the Morgan Library & Museum (225 Madison Avenue at 36th Street; tel: 212-685-0008; www.morganlibrary.org; Tue–Thur 10.30am–5pm, Fri 10.30am–9pm, Sat 10am–6pm, Sun 11am–6pm; charge). Around the turn of the 20th century, Morgan acquired entire collections from the most prominent art dealers in Europe and the United States. He bought Chinese ceramics, medieval tapestries, and Near Eastern antiquities along with Old Master paintings and drawings. He also acquired illuminated books of hours, and

handwritten letters by Thomas Jefferson, George Washington, and Napoleon, as well as manuscripts by Charles Dickens, John Keats, John Milton, and others. Equally impressive is the building, an elegant mansion with a fabulous library for Morgan, designed in the early 1900s by architect Charles McKim. The modern extension by Renzo Piano substantially increased the library's exhibition space, and added two excellent lunch options, a café, and a formal dining room. A nearby alternative for lunch is the Moroccan-themed Barbes, see ⑪②.

ROCKEFELLER CENTER

Continuing up Fifth Avenue, a left turn at West 47th Street leads into the **Diamond District ❸**, where close to $500 million in gems is traded every day, much of it by Hasidic Jews.

At 48th Street, you will find the glorious **Rockefeller Center ❹** (tours daily every 2hrs; tickets sold at the NBC Experience Store, *see right)*, a complex of 19 commercial buildings that were constructed by the financier John D. Rockefeller, Jr, in the 1930s.

Enter this vast 'city within a city' from Fifth via the **Channel Gardens**, a sloping walkway that leads to the base of the **GE Building** (30 Rockefeller Plaza), a soaring 1934 Art Deco landmark that in some ways presaged the skyscrapers to come.

Public Art

The GE Building is fronted by a sunken courtyard that becomes the venue of an outdoor restaurant during the summer and an ice-skating rink in winter. A towering Christmas tree stands here in the holiday season. The gilded statue of *Prometheus Bringing Fire to the World* is the work of Paul Manship.

Lee Lawrie's stone-relief *Genius* looms over the building's entrance, while inside the main lobby are two murals by José María Sert, *American Progress* and *Time*. Mexican muralist Diego Rivera was originally to do the murals, but the Rockefellers fired him for refusing to change a panel that depicted Bolshevik revolutionary and Soviet leader Vladimir Lenin. The unfinished mural was shrouded in canvas during the building's opening ceremony and, six months later, destroyed.

Television Tour

Before leaving, take a look in the **NBC Experience** (entrance on 49th Street; tel: 212-664-3700; www.nbcuniversalstore.com; tours 8.30am–4.30pm Mon–Thur every 30 mins, Fri–Sun every 15 mins; charge), across from the glassed-in *Today Show* studio. There are quirky interactive exhibits and a collection of

Above from far left: Bryant Park; a stunning view of Central Park from the Top of the Rock observation deck.

Breakfast Anyone? One of the most famous pre-lunch scenes in American cinema history took place on Fifth Avenue. Who can forget Audrey Hepburn as Holly Golightly, gazing in the windows of Tiffany's, Fifth Avenue at 57th Street, while munching dreamily on a flaky pastry?

Food and Drink 🍽

② BARBES
21 East 36th Street (between Fifth and Madison avenues); tel: 212-684-0215; daily L and D; $–$$
One of the city's best Moroccan restaurants has an inviting lunch menu that includes sandwiches and burgers as well as tagines.

③ ALGONQUIN HOTEL
59 West 44th Street (near Sixth Avenue); tel: 212-840-6800; daily B, L, and D; $$$
Whether it's Martinis at the Blue Bar or afternoon tea in the wood-paneled lobby, there's a sense of literary history in the space once occupied by Dorothy Parker and other members of the Round Table.

④ DB BISTRO MODERNE
55 West 44th Street (near Sixth Avenue); tel: 212-391-2400; Mon–Sat B and L, daily D; $$$$
So modern that its menu is organized by ingredients, chef Daniel Boulud's bistro is awash with Art Deco glitz and well-heeled publishing types and trendy tourists. The foie gras-and-truffle burger is typical of the kitchen's culinary surprises.

FAO Schwarz
This cavernous toy store on Fifth Avenue (at No. 767; tel: 212-644-9400) is a New York classic. For a mouthwatering selection of sweets, visit FAO Schweetz.

memorabilia from the network's 80-year history. However, the highlight is the 70-minute behind-the-scenes **NBC Studio Tour**.

Top of the Rock

Also available are tickets for the **Top of the Rock** (tel: 212-698-2000; www.topoftherocknyc.com; daily 8am–midnight, last ascent 11pm; charge), an observation deck on the 70th floor of

the GE Building. If you don't have time for the Empire State, this is a good alternative, as the lines tend to be shorter, the observation deck less crowded, and the views include Central Park – which you don't see very well from King Kong's old haunt. The observation deck is also glassed in, rather than protected by railings, so views here are less interrupted.

For a properly Art Deco setting, **Brasserie Ruhlmann**, see ⑪⑤, opposite the plaza on 50th Street, is the place. The **Rock Center Café**, see ⑪⑥, is another refueling option.

Food and Drink 🍴

⑤ BRASSERIE RUHLMANN
45 Rockefeller Plaza (between Fifth and Sixth avenues); tel: 212-974-2020; Mon–Sat L and D, Sun Br; $$–$$$
A bit of 1920s Paris in Rockefeller Center. This inviting café was named for Art Deco designer Emile-Jacques Ruhlmann and pays homage with Deco decor. Chef Laurent Tourondel gets top marks for his bistro offerings. The shady patio invites lingering.

⑥ ROCK CENTER CAFÉ
20 West 50th Street; tel: 212-332-7620; Mon–Fri B, L, and D, Sat–Sun L and D; $$
Winter views of the ice-skating rink make this a cheery place to enjoy Italian fare (the crab and risotto cakes are a standout). In summer the rink is converted to garden setting.

⑦ FIG & OLIVE
10 East 52nd Street (between Fifth and Madison avenues); tel: 212-319-2002; Mon–Sat L and D, Sun Br; $–$$$
Interesting Mediterranean menu featuring virgin olive oils, paninis, salads and tarts at lunch, More expensive for dinner, with a tasting menu at the bar.

ST PATRICK'S CATHEDRAL

Back on street level, a huge bronze sculpture of *Atlas*, also by Lee Lawrie, stands in front of the **International Building**, between 50th and 51st streets. **St Patrick's Cathedral** ❺ (daily 6.30am–8.45pm; free), on the other side of Fifth Avenue, towers over the scene. Dedicated in 1879, St Patrick's ornate neo-Gothic facade works as an intriguing counterpoint to the angular lines and smooth surfaces of the surrounding skyscrapers. Take time to admire the cathedral's interior, notably its impressive stained glass.

Just north of the Cathedral on Fifth Avenue is **Fig & Olive** ⑪⑦, another good spot for lunch.

THE PALEY CENTER FOR MEDIA

For a restful nostalgia stop, detour west half a block on 52nd Street to the **Paley Center for Media** ❻ (25 East 52nd

Street; tel: 212-621-6600; www.paley center.org; Wed–Sun noon–6pm, Thur until 8pm). Named for William Paley, former head of the CBS network, this is a rare treasure trove of 150,000 radio and television programs from their earliest days. In the fourth-floor library, you can sit at a screen and have your choice of hundreds of vintage shows, from *I Love Lucy* to *The Honeymooners*. Helpful staff will show you how to navigate. The downstairs auditorium shows films with themes such as 'Funny Women of TV.'

SHOPPING STOPS

From here Fifth Avenue is mostly devoted to commerce, although several churches do counterbalance the materialism to a degree. **Saks Fifth Avenue**, one of the country's best department stores, is across from Rockefeller Center. The super-rich can be seen gliding between Versace, Cartier, Gucci, and other shops from 51st to 57th streets.

53RD TO 56TH STREETS

The ornate facade of **St Thomas Church** ❼ – built in French Gothic style and completed in 1913 – overlooks Fifth Avenue from 53rd Street. If time allows, stop to admire the sanctuary.

Continue to the end of the next block. On the left is the **Peninsula Hotel** ❽, housed in a grand 1905 Renaissance building, which caters mostly to the corporate elite. On the right, the even grander **St Regis Hotel** ❾ *(see p.111)* is an Edwardian wedding cake of a building, adorned with marvelous

filigree and murals by Maxfield Parrish.

Across West 55th Street from the Peninsula Hotel is the stately **Fifth Avenue Presbyterian Church** ❿, built in Gothic style in 1873.

Rising from the corner of 56th Street is **Trump Tower** ⓫. Step into the lobby of this 68-story condominium complex for a glimpse of tycoon Donald Trump's signature over-the-top style, replete with gleaming brass, polished marble, and a five-story waterfall.

57TH STREET

There's shopping galore around the corner on East 57th Street, home to designers including Louis Vuitton, Chanel, and Prada. More casual are flagship stores for such well-known brands as Levi's and Nike.

Need a break? Wander into the glass-enclosed atrium of the former **IBM Building** ⓬ (590 Madison Avenue), where footsore shoppers can have a rest surrounded by modern sculpture, or enjoy a snack on the mezzanine.

GRAND ARMY PLAZA

Beyond 57th Street, it's a one-block walk past upscale department store **Bergdorf Goodman** (women's fashions are in the main store on the west side of Fifth, men's on the east) to **Grand Army Plaza** ⓭, which serves as a gateway to Central Park *(see p.46)* and the setting of the city's landmark grande dame hotel, **The Plaza** *(see p.111)*. It is now home to apartment dwellers too, but the classic style remains.

Above from far left: outside a Fifth Avenue boutique; Lee Lawrie's *Atlas* in front of St Patrick's Cathedral; the NYPD passing through; the Apple Store at Grand Army Plaza.

Apple Store
The extraordinary glass cube rising from the point at which Fifth Avenue hits the southeast corner of Grand Army Plaza is New York's flagship Apple Store (767 Fifth Avenue; tel: 212-336-1440). Head down the spiral staircase (there's an elevator for visitors with disabilities) to the lower ground floor, where, in addition to shopping, you can surf the web and check your email (for free) on any one of the computers on display 24hrs a day, 365 days a year. The Fifth Avenue store alone reportedly sells one iPod every two minutes.

TIMES SQUARE TO HERALD SQUARE

Spend a few hours around Times Square and Broadway, exploring the world's largest store and two unique museums, and purchase discount tickets if you want to end the day with a Broadway show.

Neon Jungle
Times Square's billboards aren't merely advertisements but, in the words of one prominent sign maker, 'stunning, kinetic light sculptures.' If all the neon lights in Times Square were laid end to end, they would stretch from New York City to Washington, DC.

DISTANCE 2 miles (3km)
TIME A half-day
START Times Square at corner of 42nd street
END Herald Square, Sixth Avenue and 34th–35th streets
POINTS TO NOTE
Our suggestion is to do some sightseeing, followed by a Broadway show. On Wednesday and on weekends, you could end a morning tour with lunch and a matinee, otherwise start in the afternoon to finish with an evening show. You can also divide this walk into two parts, Broadway and Sixth Avenue.

TIMES SQUARE

New York's 'Crossroads of the World,' **Times Square ❶**, spanning from 42nd to 46th streets on Broadway, swirls with irrepressible energy from the masses of people and the eye-popping neon wattage. Yet it is safer and more family-friendly than ever, since much of Broadway is now car-free.

42ND STREET

The biggest transformation is once-seedy 42nd Street, now home to

Disney theaters, movie complexes, clubs, and the always-popular **Madame Tussaud's Wax Museum ❷** (www.madametussauds.com/new york; Sun–Thur 10am–8pm, Fri–Sat 10am–10pm; charge; order online for 20 percent discount), filled with happy visitors taking snaps with the amazingly lifelike wax figures of celebrities from Brad Pitt to Abraham Lincoln.

Theater District

This area has been the heart of Manhattan's theater district for over a century, with a great heritage to be shared. Walk west half a block on 44th Street for **Shubert Alley ❸** and the 1912 Shubert Theater, headquarters for the once-famous impresario. Hopeful actors used to line up here hoping to be cast in a show. Detour half a block east at 45th Street to see the 1902 **Lyceum Theatre ❹** (149 West 45th Street), the oldest continually operating theatre, with an elegant columned Beaux Arts facade and mansard roof.

This is also the heart of media land, so look out on Broadway around 44th Street for the second-story **ABC Studio ❺**, 1500 Broadway, from

which *Good Morning America* is broadcast on weekday mornings, and the **MTV Studio** ❻, where it's not unusual to see squealing teens on the sidewalk, hoping for a glimpse of their American idols.

For available discount tickets, visit the TKTS booth at Duffy Square on **46th Street** ❼ *(see margin, right)*. The tiered red-glass staircase at the rear is a fine perch for taking in the sea of neon.

For help with tickets for future dates, stop by the **Times Square Information Center** (walk-in only;

www.timessquarenyc.org; Mon–Fri 9am–7pm, Sat–Sun 8am–8pm; free), in the old Embassy Theatre on nearby Seventh Avenue between 46th and 47th streets.

For a pitstop, there are two good options on 44th Street. **Café Un Deux Trois**, see ⑪①, a busy brasserie, is between Sixth and Seventh avenues, while **Sardi's**, see ⑪②, a longtime theatrical institution, is further west, past Broadway.

You'll see other legendary theaters as you continue up Broadway. The **1912 Palace**, near 47th Street, was a vaudeville mainstay featuring stars like George Jessel, Bob Hope, and Will Rogers. The 1925 Hammerstein's Theater between 53rd and 54th, renamed the **Ed Sullivan Theater**, presently hosts the David Letterman TV show.

AMERICAN FOLK ART MUSEUM

The second half of this walk is a change of pace, with enticing museum

Above from far left: the Great White Way; a night bus in the city that never sleeps.

Cheap Tickets
Discount tickets for same-day shows can be purchased at the TKTS booth on Duffy Square. Evening tickets: Mon–Sat 3–8pm, Tue 2–8pm, Sun 3pm–30 mins before curtain; matinee tickets: Wed, Sat 10am–2pm, Sun 11am–3pm; cash or travelers checks only. Expect long lines.

Food and Drink 🍴

① CAFÉ UN DEUX TROIS

123 West 44th Street (between Broadway and Sixth Avenue); tel: 212-354-4148; daily L and D; $$
This large, hectic pre-theater favorite is a good choice for reliable, if not spectacular, brasserie fare, notably decent *pommes frites*. Crayons and butcher paper keep fidgety kids occupied.

② SARDI'S

234 West 44th Street (between Broadway and Eighth Avenue); tel: 212-221-8440; Tue–Sun L and D; $$–$$$
Diners are surrounded by the caricatures of Broadway stars at this theater-district institution. Great for lunch or a pre-show meal.

and shopping stops. Turn right at Broadway and 53rd Street and continue east just past Sixth Avenue for the **American Folk Art Museum ❽** (45 East 53rd Street; tel: 212-265-1040; www.folkartmuseum.org; Tue–Sun 10.30am–5.30pm, Fri until 7.30pm; charge), an important and delightful collection of Naive art housed in an award-winning building.

SIXTH AVENUE

Back on Sixth Avenue heading Downtown, you are walking through a canyon of high-rise glass office buildings, a quintessential New York streetscape. Note that many of the skyscrapers, such as the Time Life Building on 50th Street, have plazas with seating to rest weary feet and watch the busy business world go by. If you are feeling hungry at this point, as well as weary, head to **Le Bon Pain**, see ⑪③. Located on Rockefeller Plaza, it is a handy place to stop for a sandwich.

On the west corner of 50th Street is **Radio City Music Hall ❾**, the city's grandest theater space *(see margin, left)*.

Continuing on Sixth Avenue, you'll know the Fox Network headquarters at 48th Street by the illuminated latest news headlines across the building, and will pass the 'Little Brazil' area, so named for its many South American restaurants, at 46th Street. **Via Brasil**, see ⑪④, is a great place to sample the cuisine.

Radio City

Radio City Music Hall is a landmark Art Deco theater known for its extravagant Christmas shows and high-kicking dancers, the Rockettes. From the massive chandeliers in the lobby to the plush scalloped auditorium, the venue is palatial. Take a tour (tel: 212-307-7171; www.radiocity.com; daily 11am–3pm; charge) to see for yourself.

PHOTOGRAPHY CENTER

The next stop is the **International Center of Photography ❿** (1114 Sixth Avenue at 43rd Street; tel: 212-857-0000; www.icp.org; Sat–Thur 10am–6pm, Fri 10am–8pm; charge), the world's largest photography museum and school. There are three cycles per year of excellent temporary exhibitions, many including photographs from the permanent collection. This covers the history of the medium but is strongest on leading 20th-century photographers such as Robert Capa, Henri Cartier-Bresson, Margaret Bourke-White, and Diane Arbus.

BRYANT PARK

Bryant Park ⓫ is a green garden oasis located behind the Public Library from 42nd Street to 40th Street. Stop here for coffee and a snack at the **Bryant Park Café**, or, for a full meal, the more upscale **Bryant Park Grill**, see ⑪⑤.

Bryant Park is the scene of much activity: a carrousel, an outdoor reading room stocked with books and magazines, and chess tables. The park also hosts the city's only free ice skating in winter.

LANDMARK ARCHITECTURE

Across from Bryant Park on 40th Street are two landmark New York buildings worth a short detour. Look up above the ground-floor shops to

appreciate **Bryant Park Studios**, 80 West 40th at the corner of Sixth Avenue. It was built in 1901 in Beaux Arts style by an artist who insisted on huge windows to capture natural light.

Such notables as the photographer Edward Steichen and the painter Fernand Léger once had studios in the building, which is currently occupied by many design firms.

The former American Standard Building at 40 West 40th Street, an early design by Raymond Hood of Rockefeller Center fame, was built in 1923–4 of dark brick topped with gold, so that when illuminated at night the building resembles a glowing radiator coil. It was recently converted into the **Bryant Park Hotel**, but the elaborate landmark facade could not be altered.

HERALD SQUARE

Now make your way to 35th Street and a chance to relax and regroup in **Herald Square ⑫**, converted into a small green city park with seating under shady umbrellas, a kiosk selling refreshments and that rare amenity, a well-maintained public bathroom. It is the perfect place to relax before heading across the street to the world's largest store.

MACY'S

Founded in 1858 on 14th Street, **Macy's ⑬** moved to this location in 1902, when it installed the first escalators seen in a department store. You can still see some of the original wooden escalators today. Nine shopping floors and a cellar store stretching for a square block will surely hold something to tempt shoppers.

If you prefer a Broadway show to shopping, Times Square is just one stop away, Uptown on the N or R subway train from 34th Street.

Food and Drink

③ LE BON PAIN
30 Rockefeller Plaza (50th Street between Fifth and Sixth avenues); tel: 212-321-5908; daily B, L, and D; $
When all you want is a good, inexpensive sandwich, this chain delivers, with orders all freshly made. You'll spot other locations all over town.

④ VIA BRASIL
34 West 46th Street (between Fifth and Sixth Avenues); tel: 212-997-1158; daily L and D; $$
On the street known as 'Little Brazil,' this is a great place to try authentic specialties including big portions of beef *feijoada*, a stew that is the Brazilian national dish. There are chicken and fish dishes, too, if you don't favour red meat.

⑤ BRYANT PARK GRILL
25 West 40th Street (at Sixth Avenue); tel: 212-840-6500; daily L and D; $$–$$$
A wall of glass and a generous terrace make the most of the park's leafy surroundings. The food lives up to the setting, with a menu of expertly grilled and roasted fish and meats.

Above from far left:
Radio City; enjoying the sunshine in Bryant Park; the distinctive facade of the Bryant Park Hotel; Macy's is a must-visit for shoppers.

Kinokuni
Even if you don't speak Japanese, you may want to browse a bit in this serene book store on Sixth Avenue between 40 and 41st streets, which also features popular anime (animation) and a variety of attractive gifts.

MUSEUM OF MODERN ART

After an $858 million expansion, the world's premier modern art museum is better placed than ever to build on its fabulous collection of Picassos, Warhols, and Pollocks, and keep pace with what's new in the visual arts.

DISTANCE N/A – the whole tour is spent in the museum
TIME A half-day
START/END MoMA
POINTS TO NOTE
The museum is closed on Tuesday. Audio players can be borrowed free of charge from a desk in the lobby.

Tickets and Talks
Joint tickets are available to both MoMA and Top of the Rock *(see p.30)*, two blocks away on 50th Street, saving 20 percent on the full price. Free gallery talks at MoMA are offered daily at 11.30am and 1.30pm. Family tours and workshops are available, too, with programs designed especially for children.

Carnegie Deli
Covering a museum of this size can feel like an endurance test, so consider having an ample breakfast or lunch before beginning. An excellent choice is the Carnegie Deli (854 Seventh Avenue at 54th Street; tel: 212-757-2245), famed for its oversize sandwiches. The museum itself has three other good options *(see p.39)*.

The **Museum of Modern Art** (MoMA; 11 West 53rd Street, between Fifth and Sixth avenues; tel: 212-708-9400; Wed–Mon 10.30am–5.30pm, Fri until 8pm; charge, free Fri 4–8pm) was a daring pioneer when it opened in 1928 and has been hugely influential in the development of modern art.

THE COLLECTION

At the heart of MoMA's collection are around 3,200 paintings and sculptures dating from the 1880s, a time that heralded the beginnings of the modern sensibility and a move away from conventional figurative representation.

In addition to these, MoMA's holdings include countless drawings and prints, books, important photo and film collections, and a notable range of functional objects that exhibit good design: from chairs to cups and saucers.

Museum Layout

Some visitors will want to head directly to the fifth floor, where the sequence of galleries dedicated to the core collection of painting and sculpture begins; it continues on the fourth floor. You will notice that this is not the sort of museum to arrange art into neat categories. Instead, the galleries flow into one another with a minimum of signage and interpretation, reflecting the museum's view that there is 'no one history of modern art.' Visitors are left to draw their own connections.

MoMA's third floor deals with photography, architecture and design, and drawings. The second floor contains the contemporary galleries, sections devoted to prints and illustrated books, and a café. On the first floor is a more formal restaurant, the museum's store, and the sculpture garden.

FIFTH FLOOR

In Gallery 1, there are are many famous Post-Impressionist works. Among them are Paul Cézanne's *Still Life with Apples* (1895–8) and *The Bather* (*c*.1885), and Vincent van Gogh's *The Starry Night* (1889) and *The Olive Trees* (1889).

The range of styles grouped together as Post-Impressionists is startling. Contrast Georges Seurat's studies in optical

effects epitomised in the seascape *Port-en-Bessin, Entrance to the Harbor* (1888) with Paul Gauguin's works showing influences of African and Polynesian culture, such as *The Moon and the Earth* (1893) and *The Seed of the Areoi* (1892). Henri Rousseau's mix of fantasy and naivety is reflected in *The Sleeping Gypsy* (1897) and *The Dream* (1910).

Pablo Picasso, Henri Matisse, and Claude Monet

The next few galleries take the visitor through the transition to Modernism. The central protagonist artistically was Pablo Picasso. Compare *Boy Leading a Horse* (1906) with *Les Demoiselles d'Avignon* (1907), which announced the arrival of Cubism. Picasso's great rival, Matisse, is also well represented. In his dreamlike *The Red Studio* (1911), the artist experiments with color and space and depicts his Paris studio as a flat red rectangle with his works on the walls.

Gallery 9 is set aside for Monet's luminous *Water Lilies*, rendered late in life at his garden in Giverny, France.

Beyond Realism

Other fifth-floor galleries chart the paths of more great names in non-figurative early 20th-century art. Here are the Cubist explorations of Georges Braque and Fernand Léger, and the abstract works of Dutch-born Piet Mondrian.

In Gallery 12, the Surrealists make good their escape from physical representation into the psychic world of dreams and the subconscious. Famous Surrealist works include Joan Miró's *The Birth of the World* (1925), Salvador Dalí's *The Persistence of Memory* (1931), with its melting clocks, and René Magritte's *The Lovers* (1928).

Edward Hopper and Andrew Wyeth

Not that all artists abandoned Realism. Edward Hopper's *House by the Railroad* (1930) was the first painting acquired by the museum. Realism was also embraced by Andrew Wyeth, whose *Christina's World* (1948) is one of MoMA's most popular works.

FOURTH FLOOR

The trail resumes in Gallery 15 on the fourth floor, where works by Adolph Gottlieb, Arshile Gorky and Lee Krasner embody individual brands of abstraction. An adjoining gallery is dominated by Francis Bacon's menacing *Painting* (1946) and Picasso's *The Charnel House* (1944–5), which suggests the first grim black-and-white newspaper accounts of the Nazi death camps.

Abstract Expressionism

Spaces devoted to members of the so-called 'New York School' start in Gallery 17 with works by Pollock, whose 'action paintings' were created by dripping paint onto large canvases laid flat on the floor. Equally arresting is Willem de Kooning's *Woman, I* (1950–2).

While these artists were developing a visual language of movement and verve, 'Color Field' painters such as Mark Rothko preferred to work with broad, even expanses of deep color, as in *Slate Blue and Brown on Plum* (1958).

Above from far left:
The False Mirror, 1928, René Magritte; MoMA's recent renovation set the art world alight; *Bathers in a Forest*, 1908, Pablo Picasso; the newest wing was designed by Japanese architect Yoshio Taniguchi.

Theaters
When your feet get tired, consider resting in one of MoMA's three theaters. Movies from a collection of 22,000 (including works by D.W. Griffith, Sergei Eisenstein, Frank Capra, Luis Buñuel, John Ford, and Alfred Hitchcock) are screened most days; inquire about viewing times in the main lobby.

MoMA Store
Some of the more everyday products on show in the design department on the third floor are still being produced today, and can be purchased in the museum's whizzy, whimsical store on the opposite (south) side of West 53rd Street.

Above from left:
browsing some of the 100,000 or so objects in the museum's collection.

Artistic Architecture
The dazzling expansion, almost doubling the size of the Museum of Modern Art, in 2004 was the first project outside his native Japan for architect Yoshio Taniguchi. His design provides soaring spaces for oversize sculptures, and natural light from wide windows and a 110ft (33.5m) sky-lit central atrium extending from the second to sixth floors. The stairwells and pathways with picture windows display art as well as providing views of the sculpture garden and of people moving to galleries through corridors across the garden.

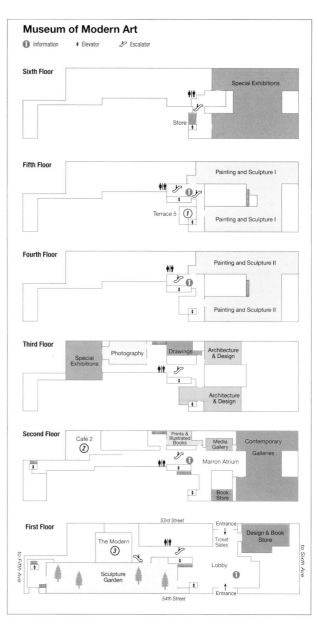

Museum of Modern Art

ⓘ Information   ✦ Elevator   ⤷ Escalator

Sixth Floor
Special Exhibitions
Store

Fifth Floor
Painting and Sculpture I
Terrace 5 ①
Painting and Sculpture I

Fourth Floor
Painting and Sculpture II
Painting and Sculpture II

Third Floor
Special Exhibitions
Photography
Drawings
Architecture & Design
Architecture & Design

Second Floor
Café 2 ②
Prints & Illustrated Books
Media Gallery
Contemporary Galleries
Marron Atrium
Book Store

First Floor
53rd Street
Entrance
Ticket Sales
Design & Book Store
The Modern ③
to Fifth Ave
to Sixth Ave
Lobby
Sculpture Garden
Entrance
54th Street

Robert Rauschenberg and Jasper Johns

Farther along are works by artists who depicted a world brimming with the detritus of consumer culture. Robert Rauschenberg's signature style was objects splattered with paint – such as his *Bed* (1955). Also found here is one of Jasper Johns's 'recontextualized' icons: the potent symbol of the American flag.

Pop Art

Andy Warhol's *Golden Marilyn* (1962) draws visitors into a large gallery (No. 23) devoted to the pop artists of the 1960s and '70s. The theme of Pop Art was consumer culture and the mass media. Warhol's *Campbell's Soup Cans* (1962) and images of celebrities highlight the commodification of images. Often working with silkscreen prints, which he produced serially, Warhol sought not only to make art out of mass-produced items but to mass-produce the art itself. Roy Lichtenstein's comic-book paintings are represented here by *Girl with Ball* (1961).

THIRD FLOOR

The design department on this floor highlights the aesthetics of functional design. There is furniture by designers including Charles Eames, Le Corbusier, and Frank Lloyd Wright, and 'everyday' items such as vacuum cleaners, kettles, computers, a 1963 Jaguar sports car, and a Bell & Howell helicopter.

The third floor also has sections on photography, architecture, and drawing. The photography department is par-

ticularly strong, as MoMA began collecting in the 1930s, well before most other major museums.

SECOND FLOOR

This floor holds the contemporary galleries, displaying the latest advances in painting, sculpture, and installation. Also here are sections devoted to illustrated books and prints. The museum contains numerous excellent examples, representing processes from woodcutting to digital printing.

FOOD AND FRESH AIR

When you are in need of refreshment, consider visiting one of the museum cafés, see ⑪① and ⑪②, or the more formal **The Modern**, see ⑪③. Afterwards, you may decide to stroll around the sculpture garden. The garden was designed by Philip Johnson in 1953 and expanded during the 2004 rebuild.

MOMA Nights

The museum presents MOMA Nights, an annual jazz concert series in the sculpture garden, on Thursday evenings in summer. Concerts move indoors in case of rain.

Food and Drink

① TERRACE 5
MoMA, Fifth Floor; Wed–Sun 11am–5pm, Fri until 7.30pm; $
This stylish café overlooking the sculpture garden is a good choice for ice cream, tarts, and a variety of light, savory dishes.

② CAFÉ 2
MoMA, Second Floor; Wed–Sun 11am–5pm, Fri until 7.30pm; $
This modern interpretation of the museum cafeteria sits guests at long wooden tables to enjoy panini, antipasti, and pasta.

③ THE MODERN
MoMA, First Floor; tel: 212-333-1220; Mon–Fri L and D, Sat D; the Bar Room Mon–Sat 11.30am–10.30pm, Sun until 9.30pm; $$$$
This dining room serves gourmet contemporary cuisine. In the Bar Room you can enjoy drinks in less formal surroundings.

UNITED NATIONS AND MIDTOWN EAST

A tour of the UN followed by a visit to several Midtown landmarks, including Grand Central Terminal, the Chrysler Building, the Waldorf-Astoria Hotel, and the Citigroup Center.

DISTANCE 2 miles (3km)

TIME A half- to full day

START UN Building

END Sony Building

POINTS TO NOTE

The closest station to the UN is Grand Central/42nd Street, four blocks west. To have lunch at the Delegate's Dining Room (weekdays only) book at least a day in advance and bring photo ID.

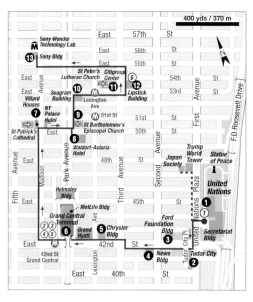

This tour covers the central part of Manhattan east of Fifth Avenue, focusing on 42nd Street, Madison Avenue, and Park Avenue, which are home to some of New York's finest architectural landmarks.

UN HEADQUARTERS

Start at the **United Nations (UN) Headquarters ❶** (First Avenue between 42nd and 48th streets; tel: 212-963-8687; www.un.org; guided tours depart from the main lobby every 30 mins, year-round Mon–Fri 9.30am–4.45pm, Mar–Dec Sat–Sun 10am–4.30pm; charge), which is situated on an 18-acre (7-hectare) campus purchased by tycoon John D. Rockefeller, Jr, and donated in 1946. Technically, this is international territory, with its own fire-fighters, police force, and postal service.

Architecture

Designed by a committee of architects led by Wallace K. Harrison and inspired by French architect Le Corbusier, the complex is dominated by the sleek glass slab of the Secretariat building. (It is, in turn, dwarfed by the neighboring 72-story **Trump World Tower**, owned by Donald Trump, *see p.31*.)

Guided Tours

The only way to see the building is by guided tour, which must be booked in advance for groups of 12 or more people. Tours start at the Visitors' Entrance, which is on First Avenue at 46th Street, and last around 45 minutes. They usually include a visit to the Security Council Chamber, the Trusteeship Council, and General Assembly Hall. Occasionally, visitors are also allowed to watch the proceedings of the General Assembly or other committees. (Ask for free tickets at the information desk for this.)

Artworks and artifacts donated by member countries are exhibited across the complex. These include murals by Fernand Léger, a stained-glass window by Marc Chagall, and ancient Indian and Egyptian artifacts.

Dining Room

Round out your visit with lunch at the **Delegates' Dining Room**, see ①, where you can rub elbows with diplomats, take in the view of the East River, and make as many trips as you like to the bufffet table.

Japan Society

A short walk a block and a half west from the UN on 47th Street and a worthwhile detour is the **Japan Society** (333 East 47th Street; tel: 212-832-1155; www.japansociety.org; Tue–Fri 11am–6pm, Sat–Sun 11am–5pm), dedicated to fostering understanding and cultural exchange between Japan and the US. Changing exhibits of Japanese arts are set against a stunning backdrop of indoor gardens, a reflecting pool, and a waterfall. Opened in 1971, the building designed by Junzo Yoshimura was the first in New York by a leading Japanese architect.

EAST 42ND STREET

Head back to the corner of 42nd Street and First Avenue, where a steep stairway festooned with banners leads to **Tudor City** ❷. This classic apartment complex dates from the 1920s, when land along the East River was used for slums and slaughterhouses; hence the windows face west toward the Hudson River.

Ford Foundation Building

At this point you can either climb the stairs or loop around the block, with both options leading to the **Ford Foundation Building** ❸, near the corner of 42nd Street and Second Avenue. Behind its sheer gray walls is a 12-story atrium thick with vegetation;

Above from far left: the Grand Concourse of Grand Central Terminal; the globe in the lobby of the News Building.

Below: the UN's Secretariat building towers above the General Assembly building; the UN flags along First Avenue are those of its member nations and are in alphabetical order from Afghanistan to Zimbabwe; *Non-Violence*, a sculpture by Fredrik Reuterswärd, was donated by the government of Luxembourg.

Food and Drink 🍴

① DELEGATES' DINING ROOM
UN Headquarters (First Avenue and 46th Street); tel: 212-963-7625; Mon–Fri L; $$
Dine with diplomats at the UN restaurant, which has a lunch buffet of ethnic cuisine and great views of the East River. Make reservations at least a day in advance. A jacket is required for men; jeans, shorts, and sneakers are prohibited. All diners must also carry picture identification.

Above from left:
the terminal's four-
faced clock; dining at
the Oyster Bar; detail
from Grand Central's
Beaux Arts facade.

constructed in 1967, the Ford was one of the first US buildings to utilize urban space in this pioneering way.

Superman

Walk west on 42nd Street to the **News Building** ❹ (220 East 42nd Street), an Art Deco skyscraper completed in 1930 and, until the mid-1990s, home to the *Daily News*, for years the nation's largest-circulation daily newspaper. When location scouts were looking for a setting to double as the office of the *Daily Planet*, the fictional paper for which Clark Kent and Lois Lane write in the *Superman* movies, this was the building they chose. Design highlights include the carved granite relief over the entrance and the giant revolving globe.

CHRYSLER BUILDING

Walk about a block west on 42nd Street to the **Chrysler Building** ❺ (405 Lexington Avenue). Commissioned by auto czar Walter Chrysler, the skyscraper, considered by many to

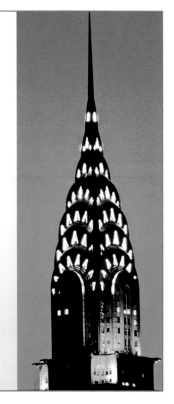

Race to the Top

When auto magnate Walter Chrysler learned in 1929 that the proposed Bank of Manhattan on Wall Street would be taller than his own unfinished eponymous skyscraper, he was determined not to be undone in his ambition to construct the world's tallest building and demanded his architect, William Van Alen, add height to the Chrysler Building's spire. Van Alen's rival was his estranged business partner Craig Severance, who, on learning of Van Alen's brief, raised the height of his own pyramid-shaped cap yet farther, and, in November 1929, held a hastily organized dedication, declaring the 925ft (282m) Wall Street building to be a world record breaker.

What Severance didn't know was that Van Alen was constructing a 180ft (60m) spire within the Chrysler Building. Shortly after Severance's announcement, workmen hoisted the spire into place, pushing the Chrysler's Building's height to 1,046ft (319m), and ending the Bank of Manhattan's moment of glory.

Victory was sweet, but short. Only a few months later, in April 1930, the Empire State Building was unveiled with the unexpected addition of a mooring mast for dirigibles (airships), surpassing the Chrysler Building by more than 200ft (60m). When the World Trade Center's Twin Towers were destroyed on September 11, 2001, the Empire State again became the city's tallest structure.

be the most beautiful in New York – if not the world – and the enduring symbol of the glamorous Art Deco era, features automotive motifs such as gargoyles inspired by radiator caps. For a few months in 1930, it was the tallest building in the world *(see box, left)*. Inside, the marble lobby, the ceiling mural by Edward Trumbull, and lavishly decorated elevator doors are in stylistic harmony with the Art Deco exterior of the building.

GRAND CENTRAL TERMINAL

Continue on 42nd Street past the Grand Hyatt Hotel to the Beaux Arts-style **Grand Central Terminal ➏**, designed by the architecture firms of Reed & Stern and Warren & Wetmore, which opened in 1913 after 10 years of construction.

Main Concourse

Enter the terminal and follow signs to the main concourse, a cavernous barrel-vaulted chamber with enormous arched windows. Note the turquoise ceiling, painted with 2,500 stars by French artist Paul Helleu; oddly, the sky was painted back to front. At the concourse's center is the rendezvous point: the information booth, crowned by an iconic clock with four faces made of opal.

At the eastern end of the main concourse is **Grand Central Market**, which shelters numerous gourmet bakers, cheesemongers, and other purveyors of specialty foods.

Lower Level and Balcony

If you are hungry, there are several options. Head to the vaulted lower level for the **Oyster Bar**, see ⑪②, one of the classic New York dining experiences. This is also the place for a coffee break or an informal meal at the lower-level **Grand Central Dining Concourse**, see ⑪③.

Carnivores should head to the balcony for **Michael Jordan's The Steakhouse NYC**, see ⑪④; for cocktails in a stylish Italianate setting, try the **Campbell Apartment**, see ⑪⑤.

Station Tours
The Municipal Art Society (tel: 212-935-3969; www.mas.org) offers guided tours (Wed 12.30pm) of Grand Central Terminal. Meet at the information booth on the main concourse.

Food and Drink

② GRAND CENTRAL OYSTER BAR & RESTAURANT
Grand Central Terminal (42nd Street and Park Avenue); tel: 212-490-6650; Mon–Sat L and D; $$
Shellfish rules at this classic Gotham eatery in the vaulted lower level of Grand Central Terminal. Oysters and other bivalves are served on the half-shell, in chowder, in pan roasts, and in 'po'boy' sandwiches.

③ GRAND CENTRAL DINING CONCOURSE
Grand Central Terminal (42nd Street and Park Avenue), Lower level; Mon–Sat B, L, and D, Sun Br, L, and AT; $
For informal meals, a pot-pourri of stalls offers American and ethnic foods, desserts, and coffee, at reasonable prices. There is ample seating nearby.

④ MICHAEL JORDAN'S THE STEAKHOUSE NYC
Grand Central Terminal (42nd Street and Park Avenue); tel: 212-655-2300; daily L and D; $$$
The basketball star's steakhouse offers slabs of dry-aged beef on a balcony overlooking Grand Central Terminal's magnificent concourse.

⑤ CAMPBELL APARTMENT
Grand Central Terminal (42nd Street and Park Avenue); tel: 212-953-0409; Mon–Sat L and D; $$
Jazz Age business magnate John W. Campbell designed this office in the station in the 13th-century Florentine style and used it for work during the day and socializing in the evenings. Restored, it is now an elegant cocktail lounge.

Four Seasons

The interior of this restaurant in the Seagram Building on 52nd Street (not to be confused with the hotel chain of the same name) has been declared a historic landmark. Art master-pieces decorate the walls of its five dining rooms, including contributions by Picasso, Miró, Pollock, and Lichtenstein.

Below: the sleek Citigroup Center.

MADISON AVENUE

When you've done Grand Central, go back to 42nd Street and turn right onto **Madison Avenue**: at this point arche-typal New York, with a skyline bristling with gleaming glass towers and streets typically jammed with taxis.

Villard Houses

At Madison and 50th Street, behind St Patrick's Cathedral *(see p.30)*, are the **Villard Houses ❼**, built in 1884 by architects McKim, Mead, and White in the style of an Italian Renaissance palace. The mansions were originally intended for journalist and railway tycoon Henry Villard, who suffered bankruptcy before construction was completed, and were later occupied by the Archdiocese of New York.

In the late 1970s, two of the Villard mansions were incorporated into the **New York Palace Hotel**, where you can now enjoy afternoon tea under a lovely vaulted ceiling created by McKim, Mead, and White.

PARK AVENUE

About a block and a half to the east, at **Park Avenue** between 49th and 50th streets, is another New York landmark, the Art Deco **Waldorf-Astoria Hotel ❽** (301 Park Avenue; *see p.111*). If you're ready for a break, pull a stool up to the long mahogany bar at the classic Bear and Bull for one of the city's best Martinis.

As you leave the Waldorf, look south down Park Avenue for a view of the floridly ornamented **Helmsley Building**, recognizable by its gold-and-green spire. Looming behind it is the **MetLife Building**, designed partly by Bauhaus founder Walter Gropius. With its absence of detailing and heavy lines, this 1963 behemoth became one of the most despised buildings in the city when it went up, blocking the vistas up and down Park Avenue.

Food and Drink

⑥ LIPSTICK CAFÉ
885 Third Avenue (near East 53rd Street); tel: 212-486-8664; Mon–Fri B and L; $$
Chef Jean-Georges Vongerichten offers breakfast and lunch at this stylish eatery in Philip Johnson's oval, granite-and-stainless-steel Lipstick Building.

A block north of the Waldorf, between 50th and 51st streets, is **St Bartholomew's Episcopal Church** ❾, a domed Byzantine-style structure built in 1919. The low-level building injects a welcome sense of proportion to the skyscrapers towering around it.

Continue a block north on Park Avenue toward the 1958 **Seagram Building** ❿, designed by Mies Van der Rohe and Philip Johnson and an early example of curtain-wall construction (in which the facade of a building does not support any load other than its own). Power lunchers congregate here at the **Four Seasons** *(see left and p.116)*, one of the city's most distinguished restaurants.

The Citigroup Center

Turn right at 53rd Street and walk another block to the **Citigroup Center** ⓫, at 601 Lexington Avenue. Completed in 1979, the building's angled roof, which was originally designed to hold solar panels, is now a distinctive feature of the Manhattan skyline. The whole aluminum-clad, 59-story structure is propped up on pillars in order to leave room below for the equally modern-looking **St Peter's Lutheran Church**, known for its upbeat 'jazz vespers' service on Sundays at 5pm. The Citigroup's atrium market houses a number of stores and restaurants.

Sony Wonder Technology Lab

As you exit Citigroup Center, pause to look at the distinctive oval **Lipstick Building** ⓬ (885 Third Avenue at 54th Street). The lobby is open to the public. If you find that you're hungry, the **Lipstick Café**, see ⓵⑥, is a good spot for an on-the-go meal.

Walk up to 55th Street, turn left, and return to Madison Avenue, where at No. 550, the **Sony Building** ⓭ (formerly the AT&T Building), designed by Philip Johnson, rises 37 stories to a so-called 'Chippendale' top, i.e. in the shape of a broken pediment, as in the style of the English cabinetmaker's storage furniture.

If you're traveling with children, consider ending the tour at the **Sony Wonder Technology Lab** (56th Street and Madison Avenue; tel: 212-833-8100; http://wondertechlab.sony.com; Tue–Sat 10am–5pm, Sun noon–5pm; free), which has four floors of interactive exhibits demonstrating the latest developments in digital entertainment.

Above from far left: Park Avenue in spring; parlor of the Royal Suite at the Waldorf-Astoria Hotel.

Below: the Sony Wonder Technology Lab.

CENTRAL PARK

The heart – some say the lungs – of Manhattan is a manmade recreation area that spans 51 blocks from 59th to 110th streets. The park covers 6 percent of Manhattan. The route below is relaxed, and a good one to do with children. Twenty-one playgrounds provide happy respites.

Above from left:
Central Park and the Upper West Side; skaters enjoy Wollman memorial Rink; on a hot day the park is filled with sunbathers; in summer, the Victorian Gardens at Wollman Memorial Rink offer kid-popular rides.

Bike Rentals
Park roads are closed to traffic on weekends, making Central Park a favorite destination for bicyclers. Rentals are available at 348 West 57th Street, near Ninth Avenue, tel: 212-664-9600; www.bikerental centralpark.com.

DISTANCE 2 miles (3.5km)
TIME A half-day
START Grand Army Plaza
END Central Park West or the Met
POINTS TO NOTE
This tour takes in the park up to the Met and could be linked with a visit to the museum (tour 6). Note that it is not advisable to wander the park at night. Free guided tours are held weekends and free audio tours are also available.

Central Park (tel: 212-7940-6564; www.centralparknyc.org; daily 6am–1am; free) was laid out by landscape architects Frederick Law Olmsted and Calvert Vaux, over almost 20 years, from 1858. Creating lush naturalistic parkland from a sparse, rocky landscape was an incredible achievement. Almost everything here, from the lawn and lakes to the forest at the north, is manmade.

Food and Drink 🍴
① BOATHOUSE
Park Drive North; tel: 212-517-2233; Apr–Nov daily L and D, Sat–Sun Br; $$$$
A great lakefront setting either in the airy, glass-fronted dining room or on the waterside terrace. Seafood is a specialty here, along with the pan-seared rack of lamb.

AROUND THE DAIRY

Enter the park at **Grand Army Plaza ❶** at Fifth Avenue and East 59th Street, where you will be confronted by Augustus Saint-Gaudens's huge gilded equestrian statue of Civil War general William Tecumseh Sherman. A trail to the west leads to a pond, which you should follow round.

From the pond, walk north to the **Wollman Memorial Rink ❷**, used from October through April as an ice-skating rink (Mon–Tue 10am–3pm, Wed–Thur 10am–10pm, Fri–Sat 10am–11pm, Sun 10am–9pm; charge) and the rest of the year as an amusement park. North of here is the **Dairy ❸**, built in 1870 to provide fresh milk and toys to city children. It is now a **visitor information center**. Check here for tours.

If you're doing the tour with children, take Transverse Road No. 1 west to the vintage **Carrousel ❹**, then retrace your steps to the Dairy and follow the path east to the **Central Park Zoo ❺** (tel: 212-439-6500; Apr–Oct Mon–Fri 10am–5pm, Sat–Sun 10am–5.30pm, Nov–Mar daily 10am–4.30pm; charge), home of polar bears, sea lions, penguins, otters, and over 100 other animal species, and the nearby **Tisch Children's Zoo ❻**.

Return toward the Dairy, then head north across Transverse Road and Park Drive to **The Mall**, a formal promenade bordered by elm trees and statues of eminent writers.

AROUND THE LAKE

The Mall leads to **Bethesda Terrace** ❼, a two-level plaza overlooking the **Lake** ❽ and the architectural centerpiece of the park. The fountain on the lower level is *Angel of the Waters* by sculptor Emma Stebbins, though it is popularly known among New Yorkers as the *Bethesda Fountain*. On the lake's northeast end is the **Loeb Boathouse** ❾, where you can rent bicycles and rowboats or, if your budget allows, enjoy a chic meal in the park's main restaurant, the **Boathouse**, see ⑪①.

From the boathouse, walk east, toward **Conservatory Water** ❿, on which model-boat enthusiasts sail radio-controlled minature yachts. Note the statues: *Alice in Wonderland* to the north of the pond, and *Hans Christian Andersen* to the west.

THE RAMBLE AND NORTH

Depending on how much more walking you want to do, you can either exit the park at Fifth Avenue and 72nd Street, or return to the Boathouse, then explore the trails that lead through the wooded **Ramble** ⓫ toward **Belvedere Castle** ⓬, which is the other side of Tranverse Road No. 2. Perched atop a rock at the edge of **Turtle Pond**, this fanciful stone structure, designed in 1865 as a folly, is now a weather station and nature center, and is a popular spot for birdwatching.

Across Turtle Pond is the **Delacorte Theatre** ⓭, focus of the Public Theater's free 'Shakespeare in the Park' Festival in the summer (tel: 212-539-8500; www.shakespeareinthepark.org). The **Shakespeare Garden** ⓮ features plants mentioned in the Bard's plays.

To exit the park, walk south along West Drive, stopping level with 72nd Street at **Strawberry Fields** ⓯, a small area dedicated to John Lennon, who was shot and killed outside **The Dakota** apartment building across from Central Park West in 1980.

Alternatively, walk east from the Shakespeare Garden for the **Metropolitan Museum of Art** ⓰ *(see p.48)*.

(see p.48)

Park Cafés

If the Boathouse tab is too steep, the Express Café next door offers breakfast, light lunches, and dinner until 8pm. Or try Le Pain Quotidien at Mineral Springs Pavilion near 69th Street, a delightful outdoor café serving breakfast and lunch. Enjoy waiter service here beneath shady umbrellas or visit the takeout section for a picnic to enjoy on the nearby Great Lawn.

Below: John Lennon in 1974; The Dakota; the Strawberry Fields memorial.

METROPOLITAN MUSEUM OF ART

The grande dame of New York's museums showcases more than 3½ million works of art from across the continents and the ages. The scale is intimidating, so let this tour guide you through the highlights.

DISTANCE N/A – the whole tour is spent within the museum
TIME A half-day
START/END The Met
POINTS TO NOTE

Note that the Met is closed on Monday and opens late on Friday and Saturday. Free gallery talks and guided tours are offered daily. See www.met museum.org or stop at the information desk in the Great Hall, where you can also rent an audio guide.

Food and Drink

① SANT AMBROEUS
1000 Madison Avenue (between 77th and 78th streets); tel: 212-570-2211; daily B, L, and D; $$
After visiting the museum, you can charge up your batteries with a shot of espresso, a focaccia or another light bite, and perhaps dessert at this Milanese café.

② THE CAFETERIA
Ground floor, Metropolitan Museum of Art; Fri–Sat L and D, Sun, Tue–Thur L; $
A self-service restaurant where hungry masses congregate for a quick bite or full meal from a range of sandwiches, salads, and a selection of hot entrees.

Met Shop
The museum store sells reproductions, posters, jewelry, note cards, and an excellent selection of art books associated with the museum's exhibits.

This tour touches on some of the most popular collections of the **Metropolitan Museum of Art** (1000 Fifth Avenue at 82nd Street; tel: 212-535-7710; www.metmuseum.org; Tue–Sun 9.30am–5.30pm, Fri–Sat until 9pm; charge), one of New York's prime attractions, drawing over 5 million visitors each year.

Depending on your starting time, fortify yourself with brunch or lunch at **Sant Ambroeus**, see ⑪①, or, if the weather is particularly sunny, go for a picnic in Central Park *(see p.46)*, directly behind the museum. Alternatively, if you're keen to get started, you could go for a quick bite at the museum's **Cafeteria**, see ⑪②, which also offers substantial dishes.

Background
The Met is a palatial gallery with a collection of paintings, sculpture, drawings, furnishings, and items of the decorative arts spanning 10,000 years of human creativity. Featuring works by artists from Bruegel to Botticelli to Van Gogh, it showcases works from nearly every civilization. Exhibits range from flints found in Egypt dating to the Lower Paleothic period (300,000–75,000 BC) up to

21st-century couture by the renowned late fashion designer Alexander McQueen.

The Met's collection was established in 1870 by a group of artists and enthusiasts who wanted an American gallery that would rival those in Europe. One of Central Park's architects, British-born Calvert Vaux, along with Jacob Wrey Mold, designed the museum's first permanent home. The current building has housed the collection since 1880, with its facade remodeled in 1926. Additions and gallery renovations are frequent.

Above from far left: the grand main entrance; in the European Sculpture Court (see p.51).

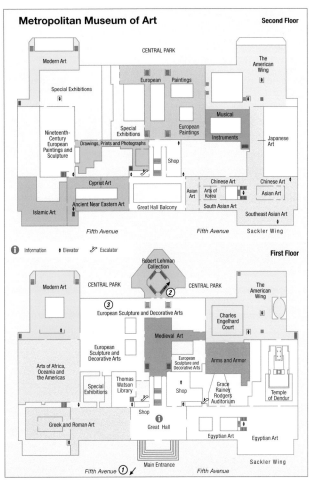

Metropolitan Museum of Art

Second Floor

CENTRAL PARK

Modern Art

Special Exhibitions

European | Paintings

Nineteenth-Century European Paintings and Sculpture

Drawings, Prints and Photographs

Special Exhibitions

European Paintings

Musical

Instruments

The American Wing

Japanese Art

Shop

Cypriot Art

Chinese Art | Chinese Art

Asian Art | Arts of Korea | Asian Art

Ancient Near Eastern Art

Great Hall Balcony

South Asian Art

Islamic Art

Southeast Asian Art

Fifth Avenue | *Fifth Avenue* | Sackler Wing

ℹ️ Information | ◆ Elevator | 〽 Escalator

First Floor

Robert Lehman Collection

Modern Art

CENTRAL PARK | ② | CENTRAL PARK

③

European Sculpture and Decorative Arts

The American Wing

Charles Engelhard Court

Medieval Art

European Sculpture and Decorative Arts

Arts of Africa, Oceania and the Americas

European Sculpture and Decorative Arts

Arms and Armor

Special Exhibitions

Thomas Watson Library

Shop

Grace Rainey Rodgers Auditorium

Temple of Dendur

Shop

Greek and Roman Art

ℹ️ Great Hall

Egyptian Art | Egyptian Art

Main Entrance

Sackler Wing

Fifth Avenue ① ↙ | *Fifth Avenue*

Naked at the Met

This is just one of five public scavenger hunts in the museum organized by Watson Adventures, who also arrange hunts at Grand Central Terminal, the American Museum of Natural History, Central Park, and other places around New York. Teams of six people (friends or strangers) scour the museum's collection for nudity in art, sculpture, and in the period rooms, attempting to be the best team to decipher the clues and finish first. No previous experience of art, or nudity, is required. Check out the website www.watsonadventures.com for details of all scavenger hunts.

The Met Goes Mod
The traditional Met didn't take easily to modern art. In one episode, a trustee gave reluctant approval for a purchase by covering his eyes and muttering, 'I just can't look.' The museum now has a sizable number of modern works, including pieces by Picasso, Matisse, O'Keeffe, and de Kooning.

FIRST FLOOR

Enter the museum and buy tickets at the aptly named **Great Hall**. The most sensible way to tour the museum is by moving in a counter-clockwise direction, so start with Egyptian art to the right of the Great Hall as you enter.

Ancient Egypt

The Met's holdings in the field of Ancient Egypt are excellent. Statues, figurines, funerary art, and coffins are arranged chronologically in a series of rooms leading to the **Temple of Dendur**, a sandstone Nubian temple from 15BC, dedicated to the goddess Isis and the god Osiris, and the physi-cian Hippocrates. Discovered around 50 miles (80km) south of Aswan, the temple had to be saved from submersion when the Aswan High Dam was built; it was presented to the United States by Egypt in 1965 in recognition of the former's help with saving other important monuments during the dam's construction.

American Wing

Behind the Egyptian rooms is the redone American Wing, which reopened in 2009 after substantial work. The multi-level collection includes furnished period rooms, a stunning loggia designed by Louis Comfort Tiffany for his Laurelton Hall home, new balcony displays of ceramics, glass, pewter, art pottery, and silver from Paul Revere to Tiffany. The Charles Engelhard Court wows with 60 examples of large-scale sculpture, mosaics, and stained glass, including works by Daniel Chester French and Augustus St Gaudens.

A new paintings gallery slated for 2011 will hold such iconic images as Emanuel Leutze's *Washington Crossing the Delaware*, Gilbert Stuart's *George Washington*, and works by Edward Hopper, James Abbott McNeill Whistler, and John Singer Sargent.

If you're ready for a break at this point, relax in the **American Wing Café**, see ⑪③, or the slightly more expensive **Petrie Court Café**, see ⑪④, in the adjacent European Sculpture Court.

Food and Drink 🍴

③ AMERICAN WING CAFÉ
First floor, American Wing, Metropolitan Museum of Art; Tue–Sun 11am–4.30pm, Fri–Sat until 8.30pm; $
Enjoy sandwiches, salads, desserts, snacks, or cocktails, with park views.

④ PETRIE COURT CAFÉ
First floor, Metropolitan Museum of Art; Tue–Sun B and L, Fri–Sat also D, AT 2.30–4.30pm; $$
The bistro fare is pricier than The Caféteria, but boasting great Central Park views.

⑤ ROOF GARDEN CAFÉ
Fifth floor, Metropolitan Museum of Art; May–late fall Fri–Sat 10am–8.30pm, Sun, Tue–Thur 10am–4.30pm; $
Order a glass of wine at the bar and enjoy the views of Central Park and the city skyline. ➜

European Art

Two floors of galleries are devoted to European sculpture, paintings, and decorative arts, plus richly appointed period rooms. The works are hung in roughly chronological fashion, starting with Giotto and his *Epiphany* (*c.*1320), followed by an unfolding of the Italian Renaissance, with highlights by Raphael, Botticelli, Tintoretto, Titian, and Veronese.

Farther along is Spanish art, showcasing the work of Velázquez, Goya, and El Greco. A section devoted to Dutch paintings includes pieces by Rembrandt and Johannes Vermeer, notably his *Young Woman with a Water Jug* (1660). A highlight of the English gallery is Thomas Gainsborough's *Boy with a Cat* (1787).

European paintings and sculpture of the 19th century are grouped together in a separate room on the second floor. Among the many Post-Impressionist works found here are Van Gogh's *Cypresses*, which he painted while confined to an asylum in 1889, and Paul Gauguin's Edenic view of South Sea life, *La Orana Maria (Hail Mary)*.

Modern Art

The Met defines 'modern art' as dating from the year 1900, and ranging over two floors in the back of the museum are exhibits depicting different artistic movements. Although the idea of Modernism was initially controversial *(see margin, left)*, the museum nevertheless compiled an impressive collection.

Sculpture highlights include an armchair by Mies van der Rohe (1927), the elegant *Bird in Space* by Constantin Brancusi (1923), and the Surrealist-inspired *Eyes* by Louise Bourgeois (1982).

Greek and Roman Art

Completing the circular route are the single-level Greek and Roman Galleries, next to the Great Hall. Opened to great fanfare in 2007, the galleries were constructed to house the Met's extensive art *c.*900 BC to the early 4th century AD. Many of the pieces had not been seen together since 1949, and bring under one roof the very foundations of Western artistic civilization.

SECOND FLOOR

As of fall 2011, the upper level of the Metropolitan will have extensive new galleries for the Arts of the Arab Lands, Turkey, Iran, Central Asia, and Later South Asia, a project eight years in the making.

The area to the right of the Great Hall's balcony contains a series of rooms showcasing Asia: exhibits from Korea, China, South and South-east Asia. Behind them are small rooms featuring Japanese art, plus the Met's excellent collection of musical instruments.

In season, from May until later fall, end this tour with a well-earned drink at the **Roof Garden Café**, see 🅷⑤, which has superb views across Central Park.

Above from far left: *Panther and Cubs* by Edward Kerneys, 1878; in the Department of Arms and Armor; the Met's collection of Islamic arts includes Anatolian, Ottoman, and Turkoman rugs; Great Hall balcony.

UPPER EAST SIDE MUSEUMS

Some of America's finest cultural treasures are housed in galleries on the stretch of Fifth Avenue between 82nd and 104th streets, dubbed 'Museum Mile.' South of here, still on the wealthy Upper East Side, are two more of the city's notable art galleries: the Whitney and the Frick Collection.

New Addition

A newcomer to the auspicious Museum Mile, the Museum for African Art, is due to open in 2011 at the corner of Fifth Avenue and East 110th street. It is the first museum to be built on the mile since 1959.

DISTANCE 2 miles (3km)
TIME A half- to full day
START El Museo del Barrio
END Frick Collection
POINT TO NOTE
Check museum opening times before deciding on which day to do this tour; most are closed at least one day a week, often Monday. A number open late on Fridays.

It would be completely exhausting to see all the museums described below in a single day, so concentrate on two or three, according to your taste. Here, we start with the northernmost museum and work south.

MUSEUM MILE

El Museo del Barrio
El Museo del Barrio ❶ (1230 Fifth Avenue at 104th Street; tel: 212-831-7272; www.elmuseo.org; Wed–Sun 11am–6pm; charge), showcasing the art and culture of Puerto Rico and Latin America, reopened in 2009 after renovations with a new facade and café and expanded galleries.

El Museo's permanent collection of over 6,500 objects spanning more than

Museum Mile Festival

A highly popular fixture in the New York cultural calendar since its inception in the 1970s, the Museum Mile Festival is held on the second Tuesday in June from 6 to 9pm and regularly attracts a crowd of more than 50,000 art-lovers and fun-seekers. The whole

of the Museum Mile, i.e. Fifth Avenue from the Metropolitan Museum north to El Museo del Barrio, is closed to traffic, and musicians, street performers, and food stalls line the route. All of the museums open for the evening, with special temporary exhibits also mounted to coincide with the festival.

Food and Drink

① SARABETH'S KITCHEN
1295 Madison Avenue (at 92nd Street); tel: 212-410-7335; daily B, L, and D; $$
To-die-for muffins, pastries, and other baked goods as well as fluffy omelets and pancakes make this an ideal breakfast (or lunch) choice for museum patrons.

800 years of Latino art includes pre-Columbian Taíno artifacts, traditional arts, 20th-century drawings, paintings, sculptures, and installations, as well as prints, photography, documentary films, and video. Changing exhibits highlight artists both past and present, while special programs offer talks, films, and poetry readings.

Museum of the City of New York

Just one block south is the **Museum of the City of New York ❷** (1220 Fifth Avenue at 103rd Street; tel: 212-534-1672; www.mcny.org; Tue–Sun 10am–5pm; charge), which chronicles the colorful story of New York from Dutch colonial times to the present. The collection encompasses myriad artifacts and artworks related to the city's ever-changing character and phenomenal growth, including historic paintings, vintage dollhouses, and much more.

Jewish Museum

Several blocks further on, the **Jewish Museum ❸** (1109 Fifth Avenue; tel: 212-423-3200; www.thejewishmuseum.org; Sat–Tue 11am–5.45pm, Thur 11am–8pm; charge) is located in a fine French Renaissance-style mansion built c.1908. Inside is an excellent collection of Judaica: art, artifacts, photographs, and antiques that tell the story of Jewish persistence in an age-old struggle. The permanent exhibition entitled *Culture and Continuity: The Jewish Journey*, mounted over two floors, illuminates more than 4,000 years of Jewish cultural history. The museum also has interesting changing exhibits.

An excellent option for brunch at this juncture is **Sarabeth's Kitchen**, see ⑪①, on Madison, one block east along 92nd Street from the Jewish Museum.

Above from far left: the central atrium of the Guggenheim Museum; detail from *Pershing Square Bridge*, 1993, by Bascove, which can be seen in the Museum of the City of New York.

Conservatory Garden

A pleasant adjunct to a museum visit is a stroll in the Conservatory Garden (daily 8am–dusk), a portion of Central Park at Fifth Avenue and 105th Street. Situated behind gates that once adorned one of the Vanderbilt mansions, this little-known oasis encompasses 6 acres (2 hectares) of manicured grounds divided into Italian, English, and French formal gardens. Guided tours are available Saturdays at 11am in the spring and summer.

Urban Palaces

Known to New Yorkers as Millionaire's Row, Fifth Avenue along Central Park has many impressive early 1900s buildings, such as the Harkness House (1 East 75th Street), the chateau-style Duke Mansion (1 East 78th Street), home to the New York University Institute of Fine Arts, and the Renaissance-style Payne Whitney house (972 Fifth Avenue), that serves as the cultural center of the French Embassy.

Below: inside the Guggenheim Museum.

Cooper-Hewitt National Design Museum

Back on Fifth Avenue, the next museum when heading south is the **Cooper-Hewitt National Design Museum ④** (2 East 91st Street; tel: 212-849-8400; www.cooperhewitt.org; Mon–Fri 10am–5pm, Sat 10am–6pm, Sun 11am–6pm; charge), a branch of the Smithsonian Institution housed in steel magnate Andrew Carnegie's 1901 mansion. The museum has excellent collections of decorative and applied arts, as well as industrial design, fulfilling its original mission as a 'visual library' of the history of style.

The museum is in the midst of a renovation which is due to be completed in 2011.

National Academy Museum

About a block and a half farther along is the **National Academy Museum and School of Fine Arts ⑤** (1083 Fifth Avenue at 89th Street; tel: 212-369-4880; www.nationalacademy.org; Wed–Thur noon–5pm, Fri–Sun 11am–6pm; charge).

This is the country's oldest artist-run organization, founded in 1825 to train artists and show their work. It upholds the custom of members submitting a self-portrait and a representative example of their work: a tradition that fortifies the academy's collection of 2,200 paintings, 240 sculptures, and 5,000 works on paper. Past members have included Frederic East Church, Winslow Homer, John Singer Sargent, and Jasper Johns.

The Guggenheim

Perhaps the greatest work of art at the **Solomon R. Guggenheim Museum** ❻ (1071 Fifth Avenue at 89th Street; tel: 212-423-3500; www.guggenheim.org; Sat–Wed 10am–5.45pm, Fri 10am–7.45pm; charge) is architect Frank Lloyd Wright's landmark spiral design, which celebrated its 50th birthday to much acclaim in 2009. At the core of the collection are the works of some of the leading artists since Modernism reared its head in the latter part of the 19th century. Many were associated with movements such as Expressionism, Cubism, and the trend toward abstraction; such painters as Klee, Kandinsky, Mondrian, Modigliani, Léger, Picasso, and Pollock. The museum recently added a gourmet restaurant, the Wright.

Neue Galerie

Three blocks south is the **Neue Galerie** ❼ (1048 Fifth Avenue at 86th Street; tel: 212-628-6200; www. neuegalerie.org; Thur–Mon 11am–6pm; charge), in a splendid mansion built in 1912–14 by architects Carrère & Hastings, whose New York Public Library *(see p.27)* reflects the same French Beaux Arts-style influence.

The museum was founded by the son and heir of cosmetics giant Estée Lauder, Ron Lauder, a former US ambassador to Austria with an interest in Germanic art and sufficiently deep pockets to indulge his passion. His collection, much of which was amassed through the Madison Avenue gallery of Serge Sabarsky, focuses on 20th-century German and Austrian art, with works by Gustav Klimt, Egon Schiele, and various Bauhaus representatives. There are also some items of decorative arts.

The museum café, see ⑪②, named after Sabarsky, is an appropriately artful place to stop for a bite.

Goethe-Institut

The **Goethe-Institut** ❽ (1014 Fifth Avenue at 83rd Street; tel: 212-439-8700; www.goethe.de/newyork), which is the New York branch of the German Cultural Institute, promoting German language and culture, is closed for renovation until 2012. Check for current conditions.

The Metropolitan Museum

The southernmost point of Museum Mile proper ends with the most

Above from far left: the elegant buildings of the Upper East Side; *The Football Players*, 1908, by Henri Rousseau in the Guggenheim Museum; the Goethe-Institut promotes German culture; taking time out on Museum Mile.

Roosevelt Island
For a little bit of outdoor adventure as a break from the museums, try visiting tiny Roosevelt Island, which parallels the Upper East Side. It has just one church, one supermarket, and lovely views of Manhattan's skyline, especially at sunset. The most enjoyable way to arrive is by the Roosevelt Island Tramway, which you can catch at Second Avenue and 60th Street near Bloomingdale's.

Food and Drink 🍴

② CAFÉ SABARSKY

1048 Fifth Avenue (at 86th Street); tel: 212-288-0665; Mon, Wed–Sun B and L, Thur–Sun D; $$–$$$

In the paneled café on the Neue Galerie's ground floor, visitors can savor the dark coffee and excellent desserts of an old Viennese-style restaurant. Replicas of period banquettes and Bentwood furniture, plus a Josef Hoffmann chandelier, provide a setting that is luxurious and distinctive. A cabaret performance and *prix-fixe* dinner are presented at the café on selected Friday evenings.

renowned of the nine museums, the **Metropolitan Museum of Art** ❾ (1000 Fifth Avenue at 82th Street; tel: 212-535-7100; www.metmuseum.org; Tue–Thur and Sun 9.30am–5.30pm, Fri and Sat 9.30am–9pm; charge). As the museum is so vast – the largest in the United States – we devote an entire tour to it *(see p.48)*.

An option for food at this point is **Candle 79**, see ⑪③, accessed by turning left onto East 79th Street.

BEYOND MUSEUM MILE

While in the mood for art, you may wish to visit the Whitney Museum or the Frick Collection; both are within walking distance.

Whitney Museum of American Art

For the **Whitney Museum of American Art** ❿ (945 Madison Avenue at 75th Street; tel: 800-944-8639; www. whitney.org; Wed–Sun 11am–6pm, Fri until 9pm; charge), continue down Fifth Avenue and turn left at 75th Street. At the corner of Madison Avenue is a cantilevered structure designed by Marcel Breuer and one of the Upper East Side's bolder architectural statements.

The Whitney was founded in 1931 by railroad heiress and artist Gertrude Vanderbilt Whitney, who, unlike her contemporaries at the Metropolitan Museum, was more interested in live Americans than dead Europeans. Rebuffed by the

Below: at the gates of the Frick mansion.

Food and Drink 🍴

③ CANDLE 79
154 East 79th Street; tel: 212-537-7179; daily L and D, Sun Br; $$$
A stylish setting for sophisticated vegetarian and vegan dishes made from organic ingredients.

④ VIAND
1011 Madison Avenue (between 78th and 79th streets); tel: 212-249-8250; daily B, L, and D; $
Attractive diner with extensive menu; try their famous turkey sandwiches.

⑤ CAFÉ BOULUD
20 East 76th Street (near Madison Avenue); tel: 212-772-2600; Tue–Sat L and D, Mon D only, Sun Br and D; $$–$$$
Renowned French-born chef Daniel Boulud combines family and regional specialties with haute cuisine to create classic French dishes.

Metropolitan, she decided to start her own museum and set herself the task of collecting the works of some of the finest American painters of the day, principally Realists such as Thomas Hart Benton, Robert Henri, and Edward Hopper.

Since then the museum has been dedicated to acquiring pieces that represent the full scope of 20th- and 21st-century art. Abstraction is well represented, particularly works by the so-called Abstract Expressionists, or New York School, who rose to dominance after World War II.

The Whitney has long prided itself on a policy of purchasing works within a year of their creation, often prior to wide recognition of the artists; a predilection for being 'ahead of the curve' that has made the museum a leader in video, film, performance art, and other modes of expression not formerly associated with museum exhibitions.

If you're hungry, try **Viand**, see ⑪④, or, for something more elegant, nearby **Café Boulud**, see ⑪⑤, on East 76th Street. The museum plans a new restaurant in 2011.

Frick Collection

Return to Fifth Avenue and wrap up your tour five blocks south at the **Frick Collection ⓫** (1 East 70th Street; tel: 212-288-0700; www.frick. org; Tue–Sat 10am–6pm, Sun 11am–5pm; charge), which occupies a mansion built in 1914 by steel magnate Henry Clay Frick. The building itself was constructed around a spectacular collection of art from the Renaissance through to the late 19th century. Intended from the beginning as a legacy to future generations, it remains one of the world's finest testaments to a connoisseur's vision.

The collection focuses on European paintings (including three Vermeers) and furnishings and represents one of the city's most successful combinations of art and environment. The ambience is one of quiet gentility. Leave plenty of time for the central courtyard, a soothing respite from the city streets.

Each year, the Frick's concert season showcases young classical musicians. Tickets must be booked in advance; see the website for dates of upcoming performances.

Above from far left: Whitney Museum; studying *Girl in Window* by Roy Lichtenstein at the Whitney.

Below: *The Comtesse d'Haussonville*, 1845, Jean-Auguste-Dominique Ingres, Frick Collection.

UPPER WEST SIDE

A tour of the Natural History Museum's dinosaur collection and the Rose Center for Earth and Space, followed by a stroll down Columbus Avenue and a look around Lincoln Center, which offers opera, ballet, and theater, and the Time Warner Center, with shops, dining, and jazz performances.

DISTANCE 1¼ miles (2km)

TIME A full day

START American Museum of Natural History

END Time Warner Center

POINTS TO NOTE

The American Museum of Natural History is an excellent attraction for children and adults alike. The museum is vast, and we advise that you concentrate on two or three sections, perhaps punctuated with a session at the museum's IMAX Theater. You may wish to end the day with a performance or gig at the Lincoln Center or Time Warner Center.

Below: the Hayden Planetarium.

The apartment buildings west of Central Park include some of the city's most distinctive, like the twin-towered San Remo, and the well-known, turreted Dakota (John Lennon was shot outside here). It's a neighborhood much appreciated by its residents. Part of this is the fact that the Upper West Side is within walking distance of three of New York's most popular attractions and some of its best food shopping.

You'll need lots of energy for this tour, so be sure to leave time for a good breakfast or brunch before starting. There are numerous restaurants in this part of town; two good options near our first stop are both northwest around 83rd Street: **Café Lalo**, see ⑪①, and **Good Enough to Eat**, see ⑪②. Alternatively, have an early lunch at the Natural History Museum's **Food Court**, see ⑪③.

AMERICAN MUSEUM OF NATURAL HISTORY

If you're traveling with children, one attraction that you shouldn't miss is the **American Museum of Natural History** ❶ (Central Park West at 79th Street; tel: 212-769-5100; www.amnh. org; daily 10am–5.45pm; charge), although there are millions of reasons for adults to visit, too. In fact, some

Above from far left:
the Lincoln Center;
Tyrannosaurus rex in
the Hall of Saurischian
Dinosaurs at the
American Museum of
Natural History.

32 million: the estimated number of artifacts and specimens housed within the museum's 25 buildings, only 2 percent of which are on display at any given time. The museum is so huge that it would be impossible to cover everything here; instead, we focus on some of the highlights.

Enter the museum via the main entrance on 79th Street; here, a statue of Theodore Roosevelt stands guard. Outside, the steps are a popular regrouping point, where families and school parties study their guidebooks and maps.

Background

Naturalist Dr Albert S. Bickmore had a passion for a natural history museum, and lobbied tirelessly for one to be established. In 1869 he succeeded in helping to found the museum, which began exhibiting its collections in Central Park's Arsenal building two years later. In 1874, US President Ulysses S. Grant laid the cornerstone for the museum's permanent home at 77th Street, although the original building was subsumed by later extensions that included a

Food and Drink 🍴

① CAFÉ LALO
201 West 83rd Street (at Amsterdam Avenue); tel: 212-496-6031; daily Br; $
A hearty brunch is served daily until 4pm at this appealing café. The bar stays open until late.

② GOOD ENOUGH TO EAT
483 Amsterdam Avenue (near 83rd Street); tel: 212-496-0163; daily B, L, and D; $
Meat loaf, pork roast, home-baked pies: comfort favorites are prepared to perfection and served in Americana-filled surroundings. The morning rush for muffins and pancakes is worth the wait.

③ MUSEUM FOOD COURT
American Museum of Natural History, lower level; daily 11am–4.45pm; $
The food at the largest restaurant in the complex is several cuts above typical museum fare, with fresh salads, sandwiches, grilled specialties, stone-oven pizzas, and an appealing choice of sweets. The barbecue and ethnic dishes are particularly tasty.

Glittering Jewels
Fans of famous gemstones should head for the Morgan Memorial Hall of Gems on the first floor of the museum. Highlights include the dazzling 563-carat Star of India sapphire *(pictured)*, donated to the museum in 1900, and the Patricia Emerald *(pictured)*, a 632-carat uncut beauty.

Above from left: the AMNH is a must for kids; Alaska brown bear diorama; the full-size skeleton of a Tyrannosaurus rex; inside one of the museum's many galleries.

Romanesque Revival facade on 77th Street and the facade on Central Park West. At the northern end of the grounds is the latest edition, which is dramatically lit at night: a glass cube housing the Rose Center for Earth and Space, which was completed in 2000.

Fourth-Floor Orientation Center

If you only have time to see one part of the museum, head straight up to the fourth floor, home to the world's largest exhibition of dinosaur fossils. Start at the **Wallach Orientation Center**, where a film narrated by actress Meryl Streep explains the modern system of 'cladistics,' which organizes living things into an evolutionary family tree made up of a series of groups with shared anatomical features.

Hall of Vertebrate Origins

Adjacent to the Orientation Center is the Hall of Vertebrate Origins. Here,

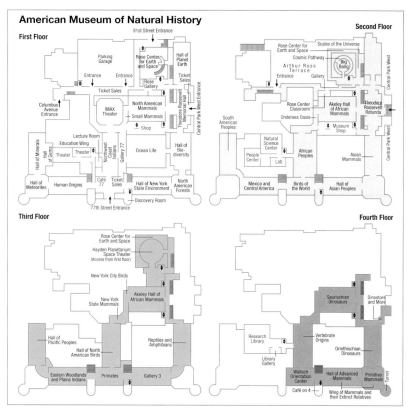

American Museum of Natural History

First Floor

81st Street Entrance
Parking Garage
Rose Center for Earth and Space
Hall of Planet Earth
Entrance / Entrance
Rose Gallery
Ticket Sales
Ticket Sales
Columbus Avenue Entrance
IMAX Theater
North American Mammals
Small Mammals
Theodore Roosevelt Memorial Hall
Central Park West Entrance
Shop
Lecture Room
Hall of Minerals
Hall of Gems
Education Wing
Theater / Theater
Northwest Coast Indians
Gallery 77
Ocean Life
Hall of Bio-diversity
Hall of Meteorites
Human Origins
Café 77
Ticket Sales
Hall of New York State Environment
North American Forests
77th Street Entrance
Discovery Room

Second Floor

Scales of the Universe
Rose Center for Earth and Space
Cosmic Pathway
Arthur Ross Terrace
Big Bang
Entrance / Gallery
Central Park West
Rose Center Classroom
Akeley Hall of African Mammals
Theodore Roosevelt Rotunda
Undersea Oasis
Museum Shop
South American Peoples
Natural Science Center
People Center / Lab
African Peoples
Asian Mammals
Central Park West
Mexico and Central America
Birds of the World
Hall of Asian Peoples

Third Floor

Rose Center for Earth and Space
Hayden Planetarium Space Theater (Access from first floor)
New York City Birds
New York State Mammals
Akeley Hall of African Mammals
Hall of Pacific Peoples
Hall of North American Birds
Reptiles and Amphibians
Eastern Woodlands and Plains Indians
Primates
Gallery 3

Fourth Floor

Saurischian Dinosaurs
Dinostore and More
Research Library
Vertebrate Origins
Ornithischian Dinosaurs
Library Gallery
Wallach Orientation Center
Hall of Advanced Mammals
Primitive Mammals
Turret
Café on 4
Wing of Mammals and their Extinct Relatives

the evolutionary tale starts about 500 million years ago. Massive armored fish such as the Dunkleosteus, whose head was encased in bony armor, appeared 360 million years ago and ruled the seas. Even more dramatic are such flying reptiles as pterosaurs and real-life sea monsters, including the ichthyosaurs.

Follow the black stripe through a corridor exhibit on the 1994 discovery of an **Oviraptor fossil** in Mongolia. This particular specimen is notable for having died while tending a nest full of eggs, the first evidence of dinosaur brooding behavior; there is also an Oviraptor egg with an intact fossil embryo still inside.

Hall of Saurischian Dinosaurs

Just around the corner, the first of two popular dinosaur halls focuses on the saurischians, or 'lizard-hipped,' dinosaurs. In the center of the hall, representing the two major branches of the saurischian family, are the towering skeletons of **Tyrannosaurus rex** and **Apatosaurus**, both repositioned with tails held aloft for balance instead of dragging on the ground to reflect the contemporary view that they were agile creatures rather than the ponderous, tail-dragging behemoths that were envisioned by early paleontologists.

The Tyrannosaurus is composed of fossils from a T. rex found in Montana in 1902 and 1908. The broken ribs, damaged vertebra, and a facial abscess were possibly sustained in battles with other animals.

Next to T. rex, munching on the tail of a sauropod, is an Allosaurus. Other large theropods (two-legged, meat-eating dinosaurs) are exhibited in displays along the side wall.

At the opposite end of the hall is the world's only display of a fossil Deinonychus, an agile predator about the size of a human. It is shown in mid-leap, ready to rip into its prey with clawed hands and – deadliest of all – the sickle-like claw on the second toe of each foot.

Hall of Ornithiscian Dinosaurs

The next hall covers the ornithiscians, dinosaurs with backward-pointing hipbones. This group includes armored and horned dinosaurs such as Stegosaurus, Ankylosaurus, and Triceratops. Also here are duckbill dinosaurs, whose rows of flat teeth were designed for grinding plant matter. The most significant specimen here is the '**Dinosaur Mummy**,' an Edmontosaurus with rare soft tissue, including a patch of skin clearly covered with tubercles similar to those of a lizard.

Early Mammals

The next two halls on the fourth floor focus on **Primitive Mammals** and **Advanced Mammals**, emphasizing the diversity of the lineage. The forebears of the mammalian line were anything but warm and fuzzy, a fact illustrated by the fossilized remains of Edaphosaurus, a large lizard-like creature with a spiny sail on its back. More familiar fossils

Above: klipspringers, small African antelope.

Above from left:
Costa Rican stone sculptures in the Hall of Mexico and Central America; the spherical Hayden Planetarium; an Aztec sun stone; one of Calle Ocho's renowned mojitos.

include those of prehistoric marsupials, giant glyptodonts, and an 8ft (2.5m) tall ground sloth.

The last gallery is dominated by creatures that our Ice Age ancestors may have hunted (or been hunted by), including cave bears, saber-toothed cats, enormous rhino-like brontotheres with shovel-shaped prongs on their snouts, and mammoths with curled tusks.

Rose Center for Earth and Space

If time permits, head for another museum highlight: the **Rose Center for Earth and Space**. This state-of-the-art science center houses the **Hayden Planetarium**, an aluminum sphere 87ft (27m) in diameter. The planetarium is split into two theaters: in the upper half is the 429-seat, dome-screened Space Theater featuring the latest Space Show, Journey to the Stars, which launches visitors through space and time to experience the life and death of the stars in our night sky. The lower half houses the Big Bang exhibit, where viewers peer down at a basin-shaped screen onto which laser images trace the beginnings of the universe.

Spiraling down from the sphere is the Heilbrun Cosmic Pathway, a dramatic ramp that ushers guests through 13 billion years of cosmic evolution. The pathway leads to the **Hall of the Universe**, a large exhibition space with displays on star formation, asteroid collisions, black holes, and other celestial phenomena. Near the center of the hall is the **Willamette Meteorite**, an eroded $15\frac{1}{2}$-ton hunk of nickel-iron forged in a distant star.

A stairway leads from the Hall of the Universe to the **Hall of Planet Earth**, which focuses on the geological forces that reshape the planet. Multimedia

Shake Shack
If you wonder why there are long lines at the corner of Columbus and 77th Street, they are for the juicy, thick Black Angus beef hamburgers at Shake Shack (daily L and D; $). Begun as a stand in Madison Square Park, the wildly popular chain, which also serves hot dogs, shakes, and custard, now has five locations and is still growing. It doesn't hurt that the prices are a rare bargain.

Detour for Food-Lovers

To see the remarkable gigantic food markets of the Upper West Side, detour two blocks west to Broadway. Zabar's, at 80th Street, is a city institution founded in 1934 and packed to the gills with cheeses, meats, coffees, and prepared foods to go. Walk south to 75th Street and Citarella, which boasts the largest seafood selection in the

city, artfully displayed like fine jewels, plus gourmet groceries, pastry, and produce. Fairway Market occupies the entire block between 74 and 73rd streets, with produce stands lining the sidewalk outside and floor-to-ceiling displays within of every imaginable kind of food. By now you will no doubt be hungry, and both Zabar's and Fairway are ready to help with their own cafés.

displays explore volcanism, plate tectonics, seismology, climatology, and other aspects of earth science.

Other Highlights

Fortunately for interested but footweary visitors, other highlights are all situated on the first floor. Just to the left of the Theodore Roosevelt Memorial Hall *(see margin, right)* is the beautifully designed **Hall of Biodiversity**, a celebration of the planet's life forms and a call for their protection. The 100ft (30m) long *Spectrum of Life* is an array of more than 1,500 models and specimens, evoking the glorious variety of life on earth. Other displays focus on endangered species and contemporary issues such as global warming, deforestation, and habitat loss.

To the left of Café on One by the 77th Street entrance is the **Hall of Human Origins**, where exhibits tell the story of *Homo sapiens*, beginning with apelike australopithecines to the fully human people of Ice Age Europe. On display are casts of a 3.5 million-year-old *Australopithecus afarensis* couple walking across the plain and 1.6 million-year-old Turkana Boy *(Homo ergaster)*.

IMAX Theater

After such a long tour of what are just the highlights, you may be ready for a rest in the spacious **IMAX Theater**, which is situated directly in the middle of the first floor. Films, usually with natural history themes and occasionally featuring museum staff on fact-finding expeditions, are screened throughout the day.

COLUMBUS AVENUE

Upon leaving the museum, consider a stroll along **Columbus Avenue ❷**, which runs north–south directly behind. The avenue and adjacent neighborhood are home to designer boutiques as well as numerous enticing restaurants and bars, including (from north to south) **Calle Ocho**, **Café Frida**, and **Alice's Tea Cup**, see 🍴④, 🍴⑤, and 🍴⑥, so take a break here if your feet are in need of rest.

Food and Drink 🍴

④ CALLE OCHO
446 Columbus Avenue (near 81st Street); tel: 212-873-5025; daily D, Sun Br; $$
Fans say the mojitos at this sexy Caribbean lounge and restaurant are the city's best. Soft multicolored lights create an alluring, grotto-like atmosphere in the bar, second home to many of the neighborhood's monied young professionals.

⑤ CAFÉ FRIDA
368 Columbus Avenue (near 77th Street); tel: 212-712-2929; daily L and D, Sun Br; $$$
Mexican favorites including enchiladas and fajitas are just the start at this friendly eatery. It also excels with less familiar regional specialties such as braised chicken in black 'mole sauce, tangy lamb, and seafood.

⑥ ALICE'S TEA CUP
102 West 73rd Street (at Columbus Avenue); tel: 212-799-3006; daily B, L, and D; $
A hundred types of tea and a dash of whimsy make this a lovely place for a light lunch and a heart to heart.

Roosevelt Memorial
The Theodore Roosevelt Memorial Hall and its four scenic dioramas pay tribute to the American president who was a pioneer in the conservation movement and had long been a supporter of this museum.

Flea Market
If you're visiting the museum on Sunday, be sure to leave time to browse the weekly Green Flea Market on Columbus Avenue between West 76th and 77th streets, where scores of vendors sell crafts, antiques, vintage clothes, and other household items, as well as fresh produce and baked goods.

Folk Art
A branch of the
American Folk Art
Museum across
from Lincoln Center
displays work from
its permanent
collection. The
gallery is at 2
Lincoln Square
(Columbus Avenue
between 65th and
66th streets).

LINCOLN CENTER

Once you've eaten enough or spent enough, continue south down Columbus Avenue to 65th Street, where Broadway also swerves to meet you. On your right is the **Lincoln Center for the Performing Arts** ❸ (guided tours every 2hrs daily, tel: 212-875-5350 for reservations; see www.lincolncenter.org for performance schedules, ticket information, and links to all the venues), where some 5 million people a year enjoy classical music, ballet, theater, and film. It is fresh from a multimillion-dollar renovation that includes a new half-price ticket booth across the street *(see p.21)*.

In the 1950s, when the city needed a new opera house and a new home for the Philharmonic, situating them within the same complex was a far-sighted idea. So was erecting a sophisticated cultural center in this part of Manhattan, best known for drug-infested 'Needle Park,' and as the location for composer Leonard Bernstein's story of gang warfare, *West Side Story*. Today, of course, this is New York's premier arts center.

The spouting fountain in the middle of the central plaza is surrounded by the glass-and-white-marble facades of Lincoln Center's three main structures. The prestigious **Metropolitan Opera** is directly in front, with two large murals by Marc Chagall behind the glass wall.

Music and Dance

To the left of the central fountain, the **David H. Koch Theater** is shared by the New York City Opera and the New York City Ballet. The third side of the plaza is occupied by **Avery Fisher Hall**, home of the New York Philharmonic and the 'Mostly Mozart' summer concert series.

Below: Lincoln Center and the Juilliard School are known for their dance troupes.

Food and Drink

⑦ BOUCHON BAKERY AND CAFE
10 Columbus Circle (near 60th Street), Third Floor; tel: 212-823-9366; Mon–Sat L and early D; $
Thomas Keller opened this informal spot to bake the bread for his five-star restaurant, Per Se, and to offer coffees, salads, sandwiches, and quiche, as well as sumptuous desserts.

⑧ DIZZY'S CLUB COCA-COLA
33 West 60th Street (near Broadway); tel: 212-258-9595; daily D; $$
The music and menu are red hot at Jazz at Lincoln Center's supper club, which dishes out Latin and Creole cuisine with a side of live jazz.

Behind Avery Fisher Hall (next to the Met) is a shady plaza and reflecting pool around which office workers gather for lunch. The bronze sculpture in the center of the pool is *Reclining Figure* by Henry Moore; set back from the plaza is the **Lincoln Center Theater**. Also within the complex are the distinguished **Juilliard School of Music**, the **Walter Reade Theater** for film, and the **Alice Tully Recital Hall**.

COLUMBUS CIRCLE

From Lincoln Center walk south down Broadway to the southwestern corner of Central Park toward **Columbus Circle ❹**.

On the north side of Columbus Circle is the **Trump International Hotel and Tower** *(see p.111)*, situated across from the gateway to Central Park. On the south side, look for the **Museum of Arts and Design** (tel: 212-299-7777; www.madmuseum.org; Tue–Sun 11am–6pm, Thur until 9pm; charge) in a distinctive building clad with terracotta panels. MAD, as it refers to itself, is dedicated to showing contemporary works in glass, metal, clay, wood, and paper.

Looming above and almost dwarfing Columbus Circle is the **Time Warner Center**, whose asymmetric glass towers look over the stately statue of explorer Christopher Columbus, for which the circle is named. The upscale stores and restaurants here played a key role in the recent regeneration of this area. The studios of TV channel **CNN** are on the third floor.

If it feels like time to refuel, stop off at **Bouchon Bakery and Cafe** on the third floor of 10 Columbus Circus, see ⑪⑦.

The Time Warner Center is also the home of **Jazz at Lincoln Center** (tel: 212-258-9800; www.jazzatlincoln center.org), with two auditoriums and **Dizzy's Club Coca-Cola**, see ⑪⑧. Visit the **Jazz Hall of Fame**, or perhaps end the day with a gig in the center's **Frederick P. Rose Hall** or cabaret in the Allen Room, accompanied with a dazzling city view through the back wall of glass.

Above from far left: Jazz at Lincoln Center, housed in the Time Warner Center, offers concerts, cabaret, and a jazz club; the lobby of the Trump International Hotel and Tower.

Building Green

The greening of Manhattan has begun. The city's first fully certified green building is Hearst Tower, just south of Columbus Circle on Eighth Avenue between 57th and 56th streets, the headquarters of the publishing giant whose magazines include *Esquire*, *Cosmopolitan*, and *House Beautiful*. Constructed atop the 1928 Art Deco Hearst building, the 46-story glass tower is designed to minimize waste and save energy. More than 90 percent of the tower's structural steel contains recycled material, as do the carpeting and furniture. A water collection system diverts rainwater to the air conditioners as well as to the three-story waterfall that cools the atrium. Sensors dim the lights when no one is present, and the tower's glass skin lets in sunlight without unwanted heat. Thanks to improved ventilation, air quality inside the building may be better than outside, which, in smoggy Midtown, leaves everyone breathing easier.

HARLEM

America's largest and most famous African-American community is enjoying a renaissance, while retaining the heritage, jazz, gospel, and soul food that make a visit special.

DISTANCE 1½ miles (2.5km)

TIME A half-day

START Strivers' Row, 138th Street

END Shabazz Market, 116th Street

POINTS TO NOTE

Take the C train to 135th Street and Frederick Douglass Boulevard to start the tour. For those who don't want to walk all the way, the No. M7 bus runs along Lenox Avenue in both directions.

Guided Tours

Guided tours are a good way to learn local history. Harlem Spirituals (tel: 212-391-0900; www. harlemspirituals.com) and Harlem Heritage Tours (tel: 212-280-7888; www.harlem heritage. com) offer some of the best, with themes such as heritage and history, gospel on Sundays, and evening jazz excursions.

Harlem's history goes from Dutch settlement to upscale residential area to mecca for African-Americans. Writers like Langston Hughes, musicians, and artists made the area famous in the late 1920s, the era known as the Harlem Renaissance. The Depression preceded decades of lean years, but recent arrivals – attracted by the architecture, history, and property prices – are changing the face of the neighborhood, although the color and flavor of old remain.

STRIVERS' ROW TO THE SCHOMBERG CENTER

From the 135th Street subway stop on Frederick Douglass Boulevard, walk north to 139th Street and turn right for the **St Nicholas Historic District ❶**, two blocks of handsome townhouses built in 1891, at the height of Harlem's residential boom. Make a loop up West 139th and down West 138th between Adam Clayton Powell Jr and Frederick Douglass boulevards to see the architecture. Prominent blacks attracted here account for the nickname Strivers' Row.

On the corner of 138th Street and Adam Clayton Powell Jr Boulevard is the impressive stone **Abyssinian Baptist Church ❷**, one of the oldest and most influential congregations in the city. On Sunday mornings at 9am and 11am, all are welcome to join the throng waiting to hear the magnificent choir.

Continue on 138th Street to Lenox Avenue and turn right to 135th Street and the **Schomburg Center for Research Into Black Culture ❸** (515 Lenox Avenue; tel: 212-491-2200; www.schomburgcenter.org; Mon–Wed noon–8pm, Thur–Fri 11am–6pm, Sat 10am–5pm; free). This is part museum, part cultural center, part library, holding the nation's largest repository of black history and artifacts.

STUDIO MUSEUM IN HARLEM

For soul food en route down Lenox Avenue, try **Sylvia's**, see ⑪①. Continue on to 125th Street and turn right to the

commercial heart of Harlem. You'll see the changes taking place as well as the sidewalk vendors and small shops of old. Visit the **Studio Museum in Harlem** ❹ (144 West 125th Street between Lenox Avenue and Adam Clayton Powell Jr Boulevard; tel: 212-864-4500; www.studiomuseum.org; Thur–Fri noon–9pm, Sat 10am–6pm, Sun noon–6pm; charge, free on Sun) to see work by contemporary black artists.

Across the street on the next block is the **Apollo Theater** ❺ (253 West 125th Street between Adam Clayton Powell Jr and Frederick Douglass boulevards; tel: 212-531-5300), instrumental in the careers of performers including Ella Fitzgerald and Stevie Wonder.

Come back to Lenox Avenue along 124th Street and detour slightly for the **Lenox Lounge** ❻ (288 Lenox Avenue between 124th and 125th streets; tel: 212-427-0253), a jazz landmark.

SHABAZZ MOSQUE AND MARKET

Continue to 116th Street for the hub of Harlem's Islamic community, marked by the green domed roof of the **Malcolm Shabazz Mosque** ❼ on the corner of Lenox Avenue, where Malcolm X once worshipped. Nearby, on West 116th Street, try **Amy Ruth's**, see ⑪ ②, for Southern comfort food.

Turn east on 116th Street for a unique shopping stop, the **Malcolm Shabazz Harlem Market** ❽. between Lenox and Fifth avenues. Past the gates of miniature minarets are stalls selling African art, drums, masks, and clothing.

Food and Drink 🍴

① SYLVIA'S
328 Malcolm X Boulevard (between 126th and 127th streets); tel: 212-996-0660; Mon–Sat B, L, and D, Sun Br and D; $–$$
Harlem's best-known eatery, always filled with tour groups. Reserve ahead.

② AMY RUTH'S
113 West 116th Street (between Lenox and Seventh avenues); tel: 212-280-8779; Tue–Sun B, L, and D, Mon L and D; $
This restaurant attracts celebrities, but the big pull is the Southern food.

Above from far left:
Lenox Avenue is co-named Malcolm X Boulevard; the Apollo Theater; brownstones in Strivers' Row; dining at Amy Ruth's.

Street Names
Remember: Frederick Douglass Boulevard = Eighth Avenue, Adam Clayton Powell Jr Boulevard = Seventh Avenue, and Malcolm X Boulevard = Sixth Avenue.

THE CLOISTERS

Far from the hustle of Midtown Manhattan is this repository of medieval culture set in a complex of reconstructed monasteries, and curated by the Metropolitan Museum of Art.

Period Garden
Gardeners will be interested to know that the Bonnefont Cloister holds one of the world's most specialized plant collections, with some 250 species used in the Middle Ages for cooking, medicine, and magic. The Trie Cloister, with its central fountain, frames a garden filled with plants typical of the European countryside: bluebells and irises from the meadows, cattails that grow along streams, and woodland primroses and violets.

DISTANCE N/A – the whole tour is spent within The Cloisters
TIME A half-day
START/END The Cloisters, Fort Tryon Park
POINTS TO NOTE
Take the M4 bus to the last stop (Fort Tryon Park–The Cloisters). Or, if you don't mind a short walk, take the A train to 190th Street, exit by elevator, and walk north along Margaret Corbin Drive for about 10 minutes. The New Leaf Café is a short walk from the museum.

Right: stained-glass panels adorn The Cloisters' galleries and reconstructed chapels.

If the city's frenetic pace is getting on your nerves, consider a serene journey to **The Cloisters** (Fort Tryon Park; tel: 212-923-3700; www.metmuseum.org; Mar–Oct 9.30am–5.15pm, Nov–Feb Tue–Sun 9.30am–4.45pm; guided tours daily at 1pm; charge). Perched on a rocky bluff overlooking the Hudson River at Manhattan's northern tip, this branch of the Metropolitan Museum of Art is dedicated to medieval art and architecture. Much of the building is reconstructed from pieces of 12th-century monasteries.

The financial force behind the institution, as with so many others in New York, was John D. Rockefeller, Jr. But the man who was really responsible was George Grey Barnard, a sculptor and collector who scoured the French countryside for church sculpture and architectural fragments. The result is an enchanting composite that evokes the hushed atmosphere of an ecclesiastical retreat. It's tranquil, fascinating, and as far away from the city as you can get without leaving Manhattan.

UPPER LEVEL

The Cloisters is on two levels. On the **upper level**, the *Unicorn Tapestries*, woven in Brussels in about 1500, have long been seen as the crown jewels of the

museum's collection. The images depict the hunt of the mythological unicorn, whose capture, death, and restoration may represent the incarnation, death, and resurrection of Jesus Christ.

Three of the five cloisters are also on this floor. Directly in front of the room containing the *Unicorn Tapestries* is the **Cuxa Cloister**, from a Benedictine monastery in southern France. The Romanesque marble capitals on the columns are characterized by intricately carved scrolling leaves, acanthus blossoms, and animals with two bodies and a common head. A fountain in the center of the enclosed garden divides the

Above from far left:
The Cloisters overlook the Hudson River; the Cuxa Cloister.

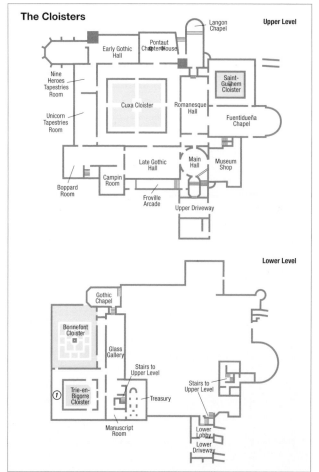

The Cloisters

Upper Level

- Langon Chapel
- Early Gothic Hall
- Pontaut Chapter House
- Nine Heroes Tapestries Room
- Cuxa Cloister
- Saint-Guilhem Cloister
- Romanesque Hall
- Fuentidueña Chapel
- Unicorn Tapestries Room
- Late Gothic Hall
- Main Hall
- Museum Shop
- Campin Room
- Boppard Room
- Froville Arcade
- Upper Driveway

Lower Level

- Gothic Chapel
- Bonnefont Cloister
- Glass Gallery
- Stairs to Upper Level
- Stairs to Upper Level
- Trie-en-Bigorre Cloister
- Treasury
- Manuscript Room
- Lower Lobby
- Lower Driveway

Serene Scenes
John D. Rockefeller, Jr, donated Fort Tryon Park to the City of New York in 1930, with the condition that some of the acres be set aside for The Cloisters. He also presented the land across the Hudson River from the museum to the state of New Jersey, so that visitors to The Cloisters would have spectacular, unimpeded views from its grounds.

Audio Tour
Lightweight audio guides are available, providing information on the history of The Cloisters, its architecture, its gardens, and some 70 works of art. The guide includes 75 stops (about 2 hours of programming).

space into four grassy quadrants, each with a fruit tree and bordered by herbs and flowers.

Romanesque Hall

Separating two of the cloisters is the **Romanesque Hall**. Visitors enter through a massive rounded arch supported by huge limestone blocks. Crafted around 1150, the arch's capitals are carved in low relief with floral and animal motifs. Across from this entrance is a mid-13th-century pointed Gothic archway from the Burgundian monastery of Moutiers-St-Jean. A third doorway, the late 12th-century Reugny Door from the Loire Valley, has a

Below: *The Unicorn in Captivity*, 1495–1505.

pointed, recessed arch. Statuary includes sculptures of Clovis, the first French Christian king, and his son Clothar.

There are two chapels off the hall. Under the altar canopy in **Langon Chapel** is a wooden sculpture of the Virgin and Child. The **Fuentidueña Chapel**, with its imposing rounded apse, was originally a part of the church of San Martín in the Spanish village of Fuentidueña, north of Madrid.

Parallel to the Fuentidueña Chapel is the French **Saint-Guilhem, Cloister**, which is from the Benedictine abbey of St-Guilhem-le-Désert, founded in 804 in southern France.

Pontaut Chapter House

Leading off the Cuxa Cloister are several impressive rooms. Just to the left is a reconstruction of the **Pontaut Chapter House** from Notre-Dame-de-Pontaut, a 12th-century abbey in southwestern France. The rectangular space has the signature thick walls and small windows of the Romanesque era.

Walking in a counterclockwise direction leads to the **Early Gothic Hall,** where the stained-glass windows are superb examples of the new style that was succeeding the Romanesque in churches throughout Europe in the 12th century. Statuary displayed here includes the sandstone *Virgin* (*c.*1250) from the cathedral in Strasbourg, and the limestone *Virgin and Child* from the Ile-de-France of the mid-14th century.

In the next room are fragments of the ***Nine Heroes Tapestries***, part of a 15th-century series of French pictorial textiles. The subjects of the tapestries

are heroes from pagan, Hebrew, and Christian history and mythology. Following on from these are the *Unicorn Tapestries* previously discussed.

Boppard and Campin Rooms

The **Boppard Room** contains ornate canopies with intricate twisting arches and leafy ornaments that frame six late Gothic stained-glass panels originally installed in a church at Boppard am Rhine. Adjacent, in the **Campin Room**, secular and religious themes are blended by 15th-century painter Robert Campin in his three-paneled *Altarpiece of the Annunciation*.

The Campin Room leads to the **Late Gothic Hall**. Sculptures dating from the latter part of the 15th century represent the Magi who visited Jesus after his birth. Parallel to the Late Gothic Hall is the third cloister, the **Froville Arcade**, built around nine pointed arches from a Benedictine priory.

LOWER LEVEL

Stairs from the upper level lead down to the **Glass Gallery**, where stained glass, sculpture, and tapestries are representative of late medieval works created for the burgeoning class of wealthy merchants and tradesmen, as well as for churches. As such, they reveal the growing secularization of European life at the close of the Middle Ages.

In the Glass Gallery are doorways leading to the other two cloisters. The **Trie-en-Bigorre Cloister** displays ornate carved capitals from the Carmelite convent and other religious orders in the Bigorre region of southwestern France, as well as from monasteries near Toulouse. If you're feeling hungry at this point, the **Trie Café** is open May to October, see .

Next door, the larger, late 13th- or early 14th-century **Bonnefont Cloister** has capitals and columns extracted from the Cistercian abbey at Bonnefont-en-Comminges. The simplicity of the capitals here is indicative of the strict asceticism of the monks, who considered ornamentation a distraction from the contemplation of God.

Gothic Chapel

The final room is the **Gothic Chapel**, where the effigy of crusader knight Jean d'Alluye, armed in chain mail with sword and shield, lies upon his tomb. There are several stained-glass windows in this chapel, as well as funerary monuments, including the tombs of the Spanish counts of Urgell.

When you've finished exploring The Cloisters, stroll through Fort Tryon Park to the **New Leaf Café**, see .

Above from far left: cloister fountain; the effigy of Jean d'Alluye in the Gothic Chapel; detail of a gargoyle; 12th-century painting *Descent of the Holy Spirit* from Meuse Valley, France.

Medieval Music
Call 212-650-2290 for information about concerts at The Cloisters. Performances are held in the 12th-century Fuentidueña Chapel and feature medieval compositions played on period instruments. Concert ticket prices include free same-day admission to the museum.

Food and Drink

① TRIE CAFÉ
The Cloisters; May–Oct Tue–Sun L; $
Visitors can enjoy sweets and sandwiches at a café in the walkway of a French cloister.

② NEW LEAF CAFÉ
Fort Tryon Park; tel: 212-568-5323; Tue–Sat L and D, Sun D, Sat–Sun Br; $$
At the southern entrance to Fort Tryon Park is this airy, oak-paneled café in a restored 1930s building, which turns out creative salads, sandwiches, and beef and chicken dishes. Live jazz on Thursday and Friday nights.

FLATIRON, SOFI, UNION SQUARE, AND CHELSEA

This route takes in some of Downtown's most innovative neighborhoods and sights: New York's first skyscraper, the Flatiron Building, buzzy Union Square, and artistic Chelsea.

DISTANCE 2½ miles (4km)
TIME A half-day
START Flatiron Building
END Hotel Chelsea
POINTS TO NOTE

The best days for this tour are Monday, Wednesday, Friday, or Saturday, when farmers come to Union Square for the Greenmarket. Note that most of Chelsea's galleries close on Monday.

Madison Square Park

This pleasant green space between Madison Avenue and Broadway from 23rd to 26th streets is a terrific place for a picnic; and the food is already supplied. The park's cute Shake Shack dishes up cheese fries, ice-cream concoctions, and what many think is the best burger in New York City.

Start this low-key, low-rise route on the east side of Broadway at 23rd Street by the Fuller Building, which is better known as the **Flatiron Building ①** because of its distinctive triangular shape. Designed by renowned Chicago architect Daniel Burnham for the awkwardly shaped plot of land dividing Broadway and Fifth Avenue at 23rd, and constructed in 1902, the 285ft (87m) edifice was the first of the city's steel-frame skyscrapers and for a time the tallest building in the world.

Rising 22 stories, the Flatiron was immortalized in 1903 in a classic black-and-white shot by the American Modernist photographer Alfred Stieglitz, who described it as looking 'like a monster steamer.'

SOFI

The neighborhood just south of the Flatiron has been dubbed 'SoFi,' for '**So**uth of **Fl**atiron.' Head south along Broadway – it's a 10-minute walk to Union Square – following a stretch once known as the 'Ladies Mile' that in the latter part of the 19th century ranged along Broadway and Sixth Avenue, from 23rd Street down to 9th Street. It is named for the number of fine department stores that operated here at that time; today, modern chains continue the fashion business.

Theodore Roosevelt Birthplace

On the walk to Union Square, you can make a left turn onto East 20th Street for the **Theodore Roosevelt Birthplace ②** (No. 28; tel: 212-260-1616; www.nps.gov/thrb; Tue–Sat 9am–5pm,

Food and Drink

① CRAFTBAR
900 Broadway (at 20th Street); tel: 212-461-4300; daily L and D, Sat–Sun Br; $$$
Craft's informal sister offers airy and spacious dining, and a vivacious bar. An eclectic menu includes tasty, simple bites, with tempting desserts.

tours hourly 10am–4pm; free), a 1920s replica of the brownstone where the 26th US president was born in 1858 and spent his boyhood. After his death in 1919 it was rebuilt and rooms were recreated to show how a wealthy family such as the Roosevelts would have lived in the mid-19th century.

If you're hungry, conveniently located on the same block, at the corner with Broadway, is **Craftbar**, see ⑪①.

UNION SQUARE

A little farther south is **Union Square** ❸, named for its location at the busy convergence of Broadway and Fourth Avenue. This was a stylish area in the mid-1850s but was abandoned by the genteel set by the turn of the century. The square was notorious in the years before World War I as a platform for political demonstrations. Rallies drew crowds through the 1930s, but the lure of radicalism dwindled, and the area went into a long decline.

However, today's Union Square brims with life, a resurgence attributable in no small degree to the **Greenmarket** (Mon, Wed, Fri, Sat 8am–6pm), the biggest and best of the city's farmers' markets, held four days a week at the square's northern end.

Adding to the regeneration has been the influx of publishers, advertising agencies, and other fashionable media firms into the area. In a recent move, *Wired* magazine made Union Square fit for WiFi, and Manhattanites with portable computers can frequently be seen leisurely surfing the web near the busy stallholders.

CHELSEA

To the west of Union Square (from 14th up to about 20th Street) is fun, sophisticated, and arty Chelsea, a favorite neighborhood for New York's gay population. It is a mix of commercial streets and leafy residential areas. Eighth Avenue is a hub for dining, especially

Above from far left: an aerial view of the Flatiron Building; famous painting reproductions for sale at a road stall near Union Square.

Below: fresh produce at the Greenmarket.

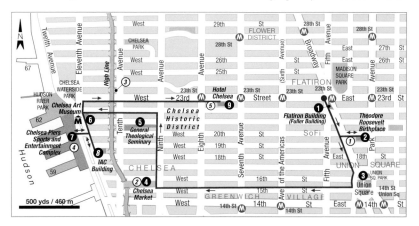

Flower District
Flower wholesalers
are clustered around
Sixth Avenue
between 26th
and 29th streets, but
be quick: the
booming real-estate
market is forcing
many shops to close.

near the Joyce Theater (175 Eighth Avenue; www.joyce.org), an important showcase for modern dance troupes. Walk west to Ninth Avenue and you'll come to **Chelsea Market** ❹ (75 Ninth Avenue, 15th to 16th streets; www.chelseamarket.com; Mon–Fri 7am–9pm, Sat 7am–7pm, Sun 8am–6pm). An ambitious renovation transformed what were 18 buildings erected between 1883 and 1930 as a Nabisco bakery turning out Saltines and Oreos into a fantastic indoor food market. Much of the original brickwork and steel remain. The interior has a waterfall and sculptured seating, around which are gourmet shops, stores, and informal restaurants, such as **Hale and Hearty Soups**, see ⑪②. Two trendy restaurants at the Market, Budakan and Morimoto, are among the city's nightime hotspots.

Chelsea Historic District

After looking around the market, walk north on Ninth Avenue into the **Chelsea Historic District**, which stretches between Eighth and Tenth avenues from 19th to 23rd streets. The land was inherited in 1813 by Clement Clarke Moore, then sold, with restrictions on development that have helped to preserve its elegant architecture. Moore is famed for writing *A Visit from St Nicholas*, which became the modern-day *'Twas the Night Before Christmas*.

On 21st Street between Ninth and Tenth avenues look for the main entrance to the 19th-century **General Theological Seminary** ❺ (175 Ninth Avenue; tel: 212-243-5150; www.gts.edu; daily 9am–5pm; free), the first seminary of the Episcopal Church. Register at the information desk, pick up a free walking tour pamphlet, and pass into an attractive tree-lined quadrangle that shelters buildings including the Chapel of the Good Shepherd and St Mark's Library.

Gallery District

When you've completed your tour of the seminary, continue up Tenth Avenue and turn left at 22nd Street for the heart of the area's gallery district. When priced out of Soho in the 1980s and 1990s, many art dealers began moving to this former industrial neighborhood, between Tenth and Eleventh avenues. Today there are some 300 galleries. The **Chelsea Art Museum** ❻ (tel: 212-255-0719; http://chelseaartmuseum.org; Tue–Sat noon–6pm, Thur until 8pm; charge), housed in an 1850 warehouse building, artfully showcases the work of interesting contemporary artists. The gallery throngs have

Gallery-Hopping

The boundaries of the Chelsea Gallery District have expanded enormously since this former industrial area first shook off its dusty image in the 1980s. It now extends roughly from 18th to 27th streets, mostly between Tenth and Eleventh avenues. Galleries are in quarters on the street or stacked up in vertical malls, where the elevator opens to a different gallery on each floor. The website www.chelseaartgalleries.com contains lists of shows and receptions. The most sociable time of year is between September and December, when it's not uncommon for the area to play host to up to six receptions on the same night. Most galleries are closed on Sunday and Monday.

brought good new restaurants to the area such as **The Red Cat**, see 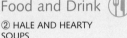③.

Chelsea Piers

If you prefer sport to art, stop by **Chelsea Piers** ❼, west across Eleventh Avenue. Until 1930 this waterfront served the Cunard and Star lines. After decades of neglect it has been reborn as a sports-and-entertainment complex stretching from 23rd to 17th streets, with roller rinks, ice rinks, a driving range, bowling alleys, batting cages, and a climbing wall. Dinner or gospel cruises are available at the marina, and the **Chelsea Brewing Company**, see ⑪④. With fine views across the river, this is a perfect place for sunsets.

IAC Building

Across Eleventh Avenue at 18th Street you can't miss the glass-clad **IAC Building** ❽. Designed by architect Frank Gehry and completed in 2007, the curvy, sail-like form was inspired by Gehry's love of boats.

Chelsea Hotel

Head up Eleventh Avenue and turn right onto 23rd Street. Between Eighth and Seventh avenues is **Hotel Chelsea** ❾ (222 West 23rd Street; tel: 212-243-3700; *see p.112*), a landmark of bohemian decadence, the second home of Beat poets, Warhol drag queens, and strung-out rock stars.

This is where poet Dylan Thomas was staying when he died in 1953; where Andy Warhol filmed *Chelsea Girls* in 1967; and where punk rocker Sid Vicious allegedly murdered his girlfriend Nancy Spungen in 1978 before dying of a drugs overdose.

Take a look at the unusual works of art (done by guests and changed at a whim) in the lobby or end this tour of Chelsea with a drink or a meal next door at **El Quijote** ⑪⑤.

Food and Drink 🍴

② HALE AND HEARTY SOUPS
Chelsea Market, 75 Ninth Avenue; tel: 212-255-2400; daily B, L, and D; $
Nothing hits the spot on a cold day like a steaming bowl of thick, flavorful soup and a slab of sourdough or seven-grain bread at this busy spot.

③ THE RED CAT
227 Tenth Avenue (between 23rd and 24th streets); tel: 212-242-1122; daily D, Tue–Sat L; $$
Gallery-hoppers gather at this welcoming, art-filled café in the heart of Chelsea's gallery district. The innovative New American chef does good things with classics like roast chicken or Atlantic salmon.

④ CHELSEA BREWING COMPANY
Chelsea Piers, West Side Highway at 20th Street; tel: 212-336-6440; daily L and D; $–$$
Choose from 20 handcrafted beers at this microbrewery on Pier 59. You can hang out at one of the long mahogany bars, or on the terrace, or enjoy a full meal in a restaurant overlooking the Hudson River.

⑤ EL QUIJOTE
226 West 23rd Street (between Seventh and Eighth avenues); tel: 212-929-1855; daily L and D; $$–$$$
A traditional Spanish mainstay next to Hotel Chelsea, with a great bargain: the lobster dinner.

Above from far left: walking the dogs; Union Square frequently hosts live events; in Union Square's Greenmarket *(see p.73)*; photography on display in the Gallery District.

High Line
The High Line, an abandoned elevated rail line transformed to a lofty park, is a pleasant respite in Chelsea. The second section, extending the park from 20th to 30th Street through Chelsea, is scheduled to open in 2011 *(see p.81)*.

GREENWICH VILLAGE

A walking tour of notable sights, shops, bars, and cafés in what was once North America's foremost bohemian neighborhood, plus a foray into the trendy precincts of the Meatpacking District.

DISTANCE 2½ miles (4km)
TIME A half- to full day
START Intersection of Bleecker and MacDougal streets
END West 14th Street and Tenth Avenue
POINTS TO NOTE
West 4th Street/Washington Square is the closest subway station to the starting point. Head south a few blocks along Sixth Avenue to reach Bleecker Street.

Bottom right: returning home from a night out in the West Village.

Start this walking tour near the intersection of Bleecker and MacDougal streets. **Caffe Reggio**, see ⑪①, is one of the last of the classic cafés where you can sip coffee at a sidewalk table and recall bygone days, when artists, anarchists, and advocates of free love ranging from Edna St Vincent Millay and e. e. cummings to Jackson Pollock, Jack Kerouac, and Bob Dylan made 'the Village' the epicenter of New York's bohemian culture. Alternatively, head west up Bleecker and turn right onto Cordelia Street for cosy **Home**, see ⑪②.

Food and Drink

① CAFFE REGGIO
119 MacDougal Street (between Bleecker and West 3rd streets); tel: 212-475-9557; daily B and L; $
Beat poets Allen Ginsberg and Jack Kerouac once hung out here; today you're more likely to find NYU students and stock-brokers, but it's still a cozy place to enjoy pastries, panini, pasta, and soups.

② HOME
20 Cornelia Street (between Bleecker and West 4th streets); tel: 212-243-9579; daily D, L, Mon–Fri, B Sat–Sun; $$
Home cooking, farm-to-table ingredients and a nice back garden make this cozy spot a local favorite. The lunch menu is served until 4pm.

③ NORTH SQUARE
103 Waverly Place (at McDougal Street); tel: 212-254-1200; daily B, Mon–Fri L and D, Sat–Sun Br; $–$$
A relaxing oasis downstairs in the Washington Square Hotel serving good New American food at good prices. Good lunch menu with prix-fix option.

WASHINGTON SQUARE

Walk three blocks up MacDougal Street to **Washington Square Park** ❶. Originally a potter's field and gathering place for public hangings, the park later became the residential center of the well-to-do New Yorkers portrayed in Henry James's classic novel *Washington Square*.

Nowadays the park serves variously as a town square, performance space, and unofficial campus for New York University, which owns most of the large modern buildings around the edges. Its everyday mix of students, chess hustlers, tourists, and carriage-pushing moms is a showcase of the social contrasts that animate the neighborhood.

On the north side of the park, serving as a gateway to Fifth Avenue, is the **Washington Arch** ❷, built in wood in 1892 to commemorate the centennial of George Washington's presidential inauguration and later replaced by this marble version. **North Square**, at the corner of Waverly Place, in the Washington Square Hotel, see ⑪③, is a good choice for lunch.

Thankfully, NYU has spared the fine townhouses on Washington Square North, which are about the only 19th-century buildings still facing the park, apart from **Judson Memorial Church** on the opposite side. The church was designed in Romanesque Revival style by architect Stanford White *(see p.78)* in the early 1890s and is associated these days with a broad range of progressive issues and events, including a series of theatrical performances, gay lectures, and art exhibits.

Above from far left: the Village was and is a center of gay culture; life imitating art in the West Village.

Jazz Standards

The Village is home to some of the world's most famous jazz clubs. First among equals is the Blue Note (131 West 3rd Street), which presents time-honored greats as well as contemporary acts. Also in the neighborhood, the Village Vanguard (178 Seventh Avenue South) cut its teeth by launching jazz royalty like Miles Davis and John Coltrane.

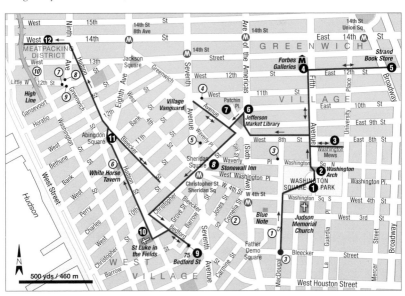

Above from left:
Washington Mews;
Macdougal Street;
Strand Book Store;
a bicycle with a
message in the
West Village.

Sex and Murder
Before there was OJ,
there was Harry K.
Thaw *(above)*.
Accused in 1906 of
shooting celebrated
architect Stanford
White, whom he
suspected (correctly)
of having seduced his
chorus-girl wife,
Thaw went on trial at
the Jefferson Market
Courthouse. The
papers called it 'the
trial of the century.'
Even President
Theodore Roosevelt
followed its progress.
In the end, Thaw was
found not guilty by
reason of insanity.

Washington Mews

Walk about half a block up Fifth Avenue to **Washington Mews ❸** (gates closed at night), a cobbled alley that runs between Fifth and University Place. The pretty little row houses here were originally built as stables for the townhouses on Washington Square North and were later converted to artist studios.

If the idea of an eclectic collection of historical curiosities interests you, make a detour a few blocks north along Fifth Avenue to the **Forbes Galleries ❹** *(see below)*. Book-lovers should visit the **Strand Book Store ❺** (three blocks east on 12th Street and Broadway; tel: 212-473-1452; www.strandbooks.com; Mon–Sat 9.30am–10.30pm, Sun 11am–10.30pm; rare book room closes at 6.20pm), a New York institution.

WEST VILLAGE

Back on Fifth Avenue, head west on 8th Street, then north on Sixth Avenue for about a block to the **Jefferson Market Library ❻**, a Gothic confection. Built as a courthouse *(see margin, left)* in 1877 and later attached to a women's prison, this Victorian landmark is now a branch of the New York Public Library *(see p.27)*. Inmates included activist Angela Davis, Catholic reformer Dorothy Day, and accused spy Ethel Rosenberg. The prison was demolished in the 1970s, and a community garden stands in its place.

Loop around the library to West 10th Street, to find tiny **Patchin Place ❼**, whose residents included playwright Eugene O'Neill, journalist John Reed, and poet e. e. cummings.

The Forbes Galleries

Malcolm Forbes, the flamboyant late publisher of *Forbes Magazine*. who had the wherewithal to indulge his passions in style, shared his tastes with the public at the very handsome Forbes Galleries (62 Fifth Avenue; www.forbesgalleries.com;

Tue–Wed, Fri–Sat, 10am–4pm). A series of rooms here – the Carrere, Hastings and Picture galleries and a Lobby Gallery – feature excellent changing exhibits of art, illustration and photography, often from private collections of members of the Forbes family. The Jewelry Gallery is one of the highlights, with rotating exhibits such as 'The Vintage Woman: A Century of Costume Jewelry in America, 1910–2010'. Thanks to the generous Mr. Forbes, the galleries offer some of the best free exhibits in New York.

Greenwich Avenue

If time permits, take a detour up **Greenwich Avenue**, which has numerous shops and restaurants. If you're in the mood for a snack, **Elephant & Castle**, see ⑪④, is No. 68, and **Tanti Baci**, see ⑪⑤, is just round the corner on West 10th Street.

Christopher Street

Double back on Greenwich Avenue and turn right at **Christopher Street**. This is the traditional center of New York's gay community. Although much of the scene has now shifted north of 14th Street, it's still worth having a stroll around. Between Waverly Place and Seventh Avenue is the **Stonewall Inn** ❽ (53 Christopher Street), site of a 1969 riot touched off by gay patrons fed up with

being roused by the police. The event is widely seen as the opening salvo in the gay rights movement. (The original bar was actually next door.)

Bedford Street

Follow Christopher across Seventh Avenue South, then turn left at **Bedford Street** into one of the quiet residential areas that make the Village such a pleasant place to live. The poet Edna St Vincent Millay lived at **75 Bedford Street** ❾, said to be Manhattan's narrowest house at just over 9ft (3m) wide.

Hudson Street

Retrace your steps on Bedford Street, turn left at Grove Street, and continue one block to **Hudson Street**. Facing the intersection is the blocky, austere

Strand Book Store
Italian author Umberto Eco describes this as his 'favorite place in America.' The owners claim to stock over 2 million volumes – from half-price review copies to $100,000 rarities. In 2007, the Strand celebrated its 80th birthday.

Food and Drink 🍴

④ ELEPHANT & CASTLE
68 Greenwich Avenue (between Perry and Seventh Avenue); tel: 212-243-1400; Mon–Fri B, L, and D, Sat–Sun Br and D; $
Tiny, sociable old-timer serving sandwiches, salads, burgers, and pub fare, plus a fine Sunday brunch. Try the dessert crepes.

⑤ TANTI BACI
163 West 10th Street (near Waverly Place); tel: 212-647-9651; daily Br, L, and D; $$
Reliable and robust pasta dishes are the mainstay at this romantic basement restaurant. The front patio is open in good weather to let in the breeze.

Left: a Macdougal Street café.

Above from left:
the eponymous
Spotted Pig (see
p.120); Bob Dylan in
Greenwich Village;
dressed to impress in
the Meatpacking
District; a notable
fashion designer on
West 14th Street.

mass of **St Luke in the Fields** ⑩, the city's third-oldest church, built in 1822.

Farther up Hudson Street, amid a cluster of boutiques, antique shops, and restaurants, is the **White Horse Tavern**, see ⑪⑥, a favorite of Welsh poet Dylan Thomas before he collapsed here in 1953 after one too many whiskeys. Dylan later died at nearby St Vincent's Hospital.

Bleecker Street

Beyond 11th Street, Hudson Street converges with a six-way intersection around cute and leafy **Abingdon Square** ⑪. This tour concludes by heading northwest up Hudson Street to the Meatpacking District, where there are some great options for eating. Before making your way there, you could make a detour by turning right on **Bleecker Street**, where you can stroll around the antique shops and boutiques that line the street all the way to Sixth Avenue.

Look, too, for pricey designer shops like **Marc Jacobs** (385 Bleecker), **Mulberry** (387 Bleecker), **Ralph Lauren** (381 Bleecker), and **Juicy Couture** (368 Bleecker), which in the last few years have been cropping up on this strip and elbowing out funky, longtime retailers, much to the consternation of locals.

Bleecker is crossed by some of Greenwich Village's prettiest side streets. **Bank Street** is particularly lovely, with its cobblestones and pastel houses, as is **Perry Street**, which is one block farther along.

MEATPACKING DISTRICT

Northwest of Abingdon Square, the Meatpacking District was formerly a neighborhood of meat wholesalers and commercial butchers that has now become one of the city's most fashionable areas.

Dylan on New York
'The city was like
some uncarved
block without any
name or shape and it
showed no favoritism.
Everything was
always new, always
changing. It was
never the same
old crowd upon
the streets'.
Bob Dylan, Chronicles,
Volume One

Right: alfresco
dining in the hip
Meatpacking District.

During the day, you can browse high-end designers; there are a number on **West 14th Street** between Ninth and Tenth avenues: **Alexander McQueen** (No. 417), **Stella McCartney** (No. 429), and **Jeffrey New York** (No. 449). If you're in need of a break, there's a clutch of restaurants around the cobbled intersection of Hudson, Gansevoort, and Little West 12th streets where you can stop for dinner or drinks; see ⑪⑦, ⑧, and ⑨.

It's a fairly laidback scene, and very different from the glitz of the nighttime hours, when thin, rich, and famous celebrities jam the restaurants and nightclubs, flashbulbs pop, and the hoi polloi gawk from behind velvet ropes.

The High Line

At the edge of the Meatpacking District, the High Line runs from Gansevoort to 20th Street between 10th and 11th avenues. This is a defunct, elevated freight railroad transformed into New York's most unusual park. Built in the early 1930s to serve upper-floor loading docks of factories and warehouses, the railroad delivered its last trainload of frozen turkeys in 1980 and was left to molder for 20 years, sprouting a natural garden of wildflowers and weeds. Seeing the potential, a group of friends successfully enlisted the city to save the tracks. The original wild plantings inspired the naturalistic landscaping along a concrete walkway that incorporates parts of the rails and the original metal fencing. It offers seating, and city and Hudson River views from a 30ft (9m) high perspective. When completed later in 2011, the High Line will extend for 1½ miles (1km) through Chelsea to 30th Street.

Just below the High Line on Washington street, the **Standard Grill**, see ⑪⑩, has good food and a great terrace.

Food and Drink

⑥ WHITE HORSE TAVERN
567 Hudson Street (at West 11th Street); tel: 212-243-9260; daily L and D; $–$$
No bar tour of Greenwich Village is complete without visiting this historic watering hole, a favorite of students and assorted literati ever since Welsh poet Dylan Thomas, following his own advice, pulled up a barstool and went most ungently into that good night.

⑦ PARADOU
8 Little West 12th Street (near Ninth Avenue); tel: 212-463-8345; daily D, Sat–Sun Br; $–$$
In good weather, ask for a table in the garden at this inviting little bistro serving French wine and light Provençal fare.

⑧ PASTIS
9 Ninth Avenue (at Little West 12th Street); tel: 212-929-4844; daily B and D, Mon–Fri L, Sat–Sun Br; $$–$$$$
Long one of the most popular eateries in the Meatpacking District, the air around Pastis buzzes with beautiful people, limos, and taxis. In spite of this, it retains the feel of an old-fashioned brasserie (with furnishings brought over from Europe).

⑨ 5 NINTH
5 Ninth Avenue (between Gansevoort and Little West 12th Street); tel: 212-929-9460; daily L and D, Sat–Sun Br; $–$$
A refuge from the busy Meatpacking scene, this tri-level 1800s townhouse with a back-garden retreat serves seasonal New American fare. The late lunch menu from 3.30–5.30pm can be handy if you've had a late breakfast.

⑩ STANDARD GRILL
Standard Hotel, 846 Washington Street (at 13th Street); tel: 212-645-4100; daily B, L, and D, Sat–Sun Br; $–$$
A unique location below the High Line and an excellent chef serving up American favorites make for a popular addition to the neighborhood. The outdoor terrace is a fine place for a drink at the end of the day.

SOHO AND TRIBECA

These neighborhoods are the very epitome of post-industrial chic. They are urban playgrounds known the world over for cast-iron architecture, stylish boutiques, loft living, and fantastic food.

Conceptual Art
Soho is the location of two long-term installations by artist Walter De Maria: *The Broken Kilometer*, a conceptual piece composed of 500 polished brass rods arranged in three rows on the floor of a loft at 393 West Broadway, and the *New York Earth Room*, which, true to its name, is a room at 141 Wooster Street filled with 250 cubic yards (191 cubic meters) of soil.

Below: Soho boutique signs.

DISTANCE 2¼ miles (3.5km)
TIME A half- to full day
START West Broadway
END Tribeca Film Center
POINTS TO NOTE
The nearest subway stations to the starting point are Prince Street or Spring Street A, C, E. You may wish to build in some time during the tour for shopping in Soho. The tour ends at Tribeca, a great area for dining.

The old industrial neighborhood of Soho (**So**uth of **Ho**uston) was invaded by artists in the 1960s and soon after blossomed into a mecca of avant-garde culture. The artists, however, were soon priced out and most of the galleries have moved on, many of them to Chelsea. Today's neighborhood is devoted far more to shopping than to art.

This tour leads you through a few hotspots, though any number of distractions might lure you off the track. Soho's streets are narrow and the crowds can be daunting, especially on weekends, when many New Yorkers like to brunch and browse, so don't expect to zip through. If you're a serious shopper, you can easily spend a day strolling from one boutique to another. If you're here only to check out the scene, half a day should be fine.

WEST BROADWAY

Start your tour at **West Broadway** ❶ near Houston Street. West Broadway is Soho's main drag and is lined with high-end boutiques including American giants **DKNY** (No. 420), **Ralph Lauren** (No. 381), and **Tommy Hilfiger** (No. 372), as well as European designers **Alberta Ferretti** (No. 452) and **Giorgio Armani** (No. 410).

PRINCE STREET

The shopping district spills over into the cross streets, especially **Prince Street** ❷, which hosts **J. Crew** (No. 99), **Miu Miu** (No. 100), **Club Monaco** (No. 121), **Coach** (No. 143), and others.

While you're browsing, take a moment to admire two fine buildings at Prince and Greene streets: **112 Prince Street**, which on its eastern face has an extraordinary *trompe l'œil* mural by artist Richard Haas, and, on the opposite corner, **109 Prince Street**, a very handsome five-story edifice with a cast-iron facade that now houses Italian fashion label **Replay**.

In a former post office a little farther on is Apple's stylish **Station A** (103 Prince Street). Fight your way through the mob to try the latest iPods, iPhones, and other new gadgets. Farther along, at

the corner of Mercer Street, is the **Mercer Hotel** (147 Mercer Street; *see p.115*), a trendy boutique hotel in a beautiful Romanesque Revival building. Beneath the hotel is the **Mercer Kitchen**, see ⑪①. Other good eateries, like **Fanelli Cafe**, see ⑪②, are nearby.

GREENE STREET

Retrace your steps to West Broadway and turn left. Browse the shops down to Broome Street, detouring after one block, right down Spring Street, for hot food at **Bistro Les Amis**, see ⑪③, if sustenance is required. Turn left at Broome and continue to **Greene Street** ❸. In the late 19th century, this was the center of a notorious red-light dis-

trict, where brothels conducted business behind shuttered windows. Now the same windows attract a different sort of browser – those who gaze longingly at the latest designs by **Viviene Tam** (No. 99) and **Hugo Boss** (No. 132).

Soho Historic Cast Iron District

Greene Street is also the heart of the **Soho Historic Cast Iron District**. Most of the structures here were constructed in the mid- to late 1800s, when manufacturers moved into the neighborhood and needed to create industrial

Above from far left: lunching ladies; find seasonal food at the Savoy *(see p.121)*; Fanelli Cafe; hanging on a Soho stoop.

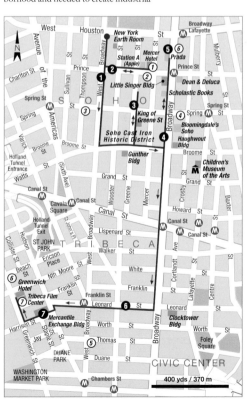

Food and Drink 🍴

① MERCER KITCHEN
99 Prince Street (at Mercer Street); tel: 212-966-5454; daily B, L, and D; $$$$
Models and movie stars flock to this slick restaurant for a taste of celebrity chef Jean-Georges Vongerichten's 'everyday food.'

② FANELLI CAFE
94 Prince Street (at Mercer Street); tel: 212-226-9412; daily B, L, and D; $
This holdover from Soho's industrial past still has the homey vibe of a neighborhood tavern. The kitchen knocks out a great burger.

③ BISTRO LES AMIS
180 Spring Street (at Thompson Street); tel: 212-289-0997; daily L and D; $–$$
All the bistro classics plus pastas and salads are served at this friendly longtime neighborhood favourite.

Above from left:
cast-iron columns frame the windows of Prada; shooting pool in a Tribeca bar.

Children's Museum of the Arts
Brightly painted windows mark the entrance to a space that is part museum, part art studio. Here children learn by becoming artists. Everything is built half-size. Parents may feel a bit cramped, but kids are instantly at home, plunging into fingerpaints, clay, collages, and costumes (182 Lafayette Street, near Broome Street; tel: 212-274-0986; www.cmany.com; Wed–Sun noon–5pm; charge).

Below: a Tribeca musical mecca.

spaces quickly. There was no electricity, of course, so it was necessary for windows to admit a maximum of light. With rear walls often facing gloomy alleys, the only place sunlight could enter was through voluminous front windows. The solution to problems over expense came in the form of buildings with pre-cast iron facades that could be assembled on site. And since casting iron requires less labor than sculpting stone, the facades could be quite ornate.

The prominent **Gunther Building** at the corner of Greene and Broome streets is especially noteworthy. It was built in 1872 as a showroom and warehouse for fur dealer William Gunther and now serves as loft and gallery space.

Farther up Greene is the so-called **King of Greene Street** (72–76 Greene Street), a splendid edifice built in 1872 in Second Empire style for dry-goods mogul Gardner Colby.

BROADWAY

Take your time exploring Greene Street before returning to Broome Street and walking one block east to **Broadway ❹**. Pause here for a look at the landmark **Haughwout Building** (488–492 Broadway), a palazzo with five stories of arched windows, fluted columns, and prominent cornices, all rendered in cast iron. Built in 1857 for china dealer Eder V. Haughwout, the building was the first to install the newfangled 'safety elevator' invented by Elisha Otis, a development that opened the way for the skyscrapers that would eventually dominate Manhattan's skyline.

Bloomingdale's and Beyond

Despite the presence of a handful of tony stores, Broadway tends to appeal to shoppers with more mainstream tastes than West Broadway. Even smart **Bloomingdale's** (504 Broadway, near Broome Street), which opened its first branch in Soho in 2004, caters to young, mid-market customers.

If you're traveling with kids, be sure to stop at **Scholastic Books** (557 Broadway), a huge, colorful retail space opened by the publisher of the Harry Potter series and scores of other well-known children's titles.

A few steps away is the landmark **Little Singer Building** (561 Broadway), a 12-story confection of terracotta, steel, and wrought-iron tracery built in 1904. The first floor is occupied by Kate's Paperie, a purveyor of fine stationery.

Dean & Deluca

Across the street, gourmet shop **Dean & Deluca** (560 Broadway) lures foodies from throughout the city. The stand-up coffee bar is a good place for a snack, although the line of caffeine-starved New Yorkers can be fairly long.

Prada

Across Prince Street, in a building once occupied by a branch of the Guggenheim Museum, is fashion temple **Prada ❺** (575 Broadway), which has redesigned the interior in the shape of a half-pipe connecting the first and second floors. It's worth a look inside even if you can't afford the merchandise.

Once you've had your fill of shopping, seek out one of the area's many inviting bars or restaurants, such as **Balthazar**, see ④.

TRIBECA

Head back down Broadway for 10 blocks until you reach Leonard Street. In the late 1970s, artists in search of lower rents migrated south from Soho to **Tribeca** (the **Tri**angle **Be**low **Ca**nal). An eclectic blend of renovated warehouses, Corinthian columns, condo towers, and narrow streets, Tribeca's attractions can easily be covered in a morning, leaving lots of time to do what Tribeca does best – indulge in eating. Some of Manhattan's best (and most expensive) bars and restaurants are here, but savvy visitors can soak up the atmosphere at a fraction of the cost by sampling a meal at lunch.

Leonard Street

Some of Tribeca's finest architecture is on **Leonard Street** ❻. Just to the east, the **Clocktower Building** (No. 108) is the former New York Life Insurance Building, remodeled by Stanford White in 1898.

Eating Options

Two blocks south of Leonard Street on West Broadway Street is the restaurant **Odeon**, see ⑪⑤. Leonard ends at Hudson Street. On the corner of Hudson and Harrison is the ornate **Mercantile Exchange Building** ❼, built in 1884 as the trading center for the egg and butter business. **Wichcraft**,

see ⑪⑥, is on the corner of Harrison and Greenwich.

Walk half a block west on Harrison, then two blocks north on Greenwich to the **Tribeca Film Center**, the offices of actor Robert De Niro and the hub of the Tribeca Film Festival. Although the center is closed to visitors, you can try your hand at power lunching in the **Tribeca Grill**, see ⑪⑦. De Niro was also involved in planning the rustic-elegant **Greenwich Hotel** *(see p.115)* on this block, built of faded handmade bricks to blend into the area, and furnished with Moroccan tiles, old wood beams, antique Asian art, and paintings by De Niro's father.

Urban Bazaar
Canal Street, Soho's southern boundary, is an urban bazaar crammed with street vendors and discount shops hawking everything from toys and trinkets to CDs, DVDs, electronics, jewelry, and industrial odds and ends.

Food and Drink

④ BALTHAZAR
80 Spring Street (near Crosby Street); tel: 212-965-1414; daily B and D, Mon–Fri L, Sat–Sun Br; $$$
Parisian-style brasserie; hard to imagine Soho without it.

⑤ ODEON
145 W. Broadway (at Duane and Thomas streets); tel: 212-233-0507; Mon–Fri L, daily D, Sat–Sun Br; $$$
One of the first Tribeca hotspots, this Art Deco brasserie has been a mainstay ever since Warhol and Basquiat used to drop by. It's open from 9am on weekends (noon weekdays) for dining; enjoy fewer crowds earlier in the day.

⑥ WICHCRAFT
397 Greenwich (at Harrison Street), Tribeca; 586 Broadway (at Prince Street), Soho; daily B and L, early D; $
This handy mini-chain by star chef Tom Colichio (Craft) serves up gourmet sandwiches and paninis, plus a breakfast sandwich all day.

⑦ TRIBECA GRILL
375 Greenwich Street (at Crosby Street); tel: 212-941-3900; Mon–Fri and Sun L and D, Sat D only; $$$
Co-owned by actor Robert De Niro and chef Drew Nieporent, customers flock here in the hope of seeing celebs from the Tribeca Film Center talking 'back story' and making deals.

EAST VILLAGE AND LOWER EAST SIDE

Take a stroll around St Mark's Place in the East Village, go shopping for new fashions in NoLita, check out the delis and boutiques of the Lower East Side, and take a tour of the Tenement Museum.

East Side Theaters
As well as the Public, the Orpheum, and the Astor Place theaters, the East Village is home to the Bowery Poetry Club, and PS (Performance Space) 122.

Music Venues
If you're into music, clubs such as the Mercury Lounge (217 East Houston Street), Arlene's Grocery (95 Stanton Street), and the Bowery Ballroom (6 Delancey Street; *pictured*), showcase indie bands nearly every night.

DISTANCE 2½ miles (4km)
TIME A half-day
START St Mark's-in-the-Bowery
END Orchard Street
POINTS TO NOTE
The best day to do the tour is Sunday, when the Orchard Street Market takes place. Whichever day you choose, be sure to book well in advance for the Tenement Museum.

This part of Manhattan is a series of neighborhoods that overlap and bump up next to each other in a convivial and vibrant way. Specific borders are difficult to define. What these areas have shared historically, aside from proximity, is a high-spirited funkiness. Gentrification is changing the mood, however. Today, these neighborhoods boast a growing number of top restaurants and boutiques that appeal to the young and hip. Take a stroll or have a meal and you'll see what we mean.

If you wish to fortify yourself with coffee and cake before setting off, try **Veniero's Pasticceria**, see ①①, a short walk from the starting point on East 11th Street.

EAST VILLAGE

The tour starts in the **East Village**, which, even after years of gentrification, still has a bit of raw bohemian quality. In the late 1960s, this was the epicenter of East Coast counter-culture, where Andy Warhol presented Velvet Underground 'happenings' and the scene at nightclubs like the infamous Electric Circus were heavily seasoned with psychedelic lights and hallucinogens.

But the East Village is much older than this. The church of **St Mark's-in-the-Bowery** ❶, where this tour begins, was built in 1799 on land that belonged to Peter Stuyvesant, the last Dutch governor of New York. Stuyvesant is buried in a nearby cemetery.

The red-brick Anglo-Italianate houses across from the church on East 10th Street and on Stuyvesant Street, which veers off at an angle from Second Avenue, form the heart of the **St Mark's Historic District**, dating from the 18th and 19th centuries.

Cooper Square

At the end of Stuyvesant Street you will emerge onto **Cooper Square**. Ahead is an immense brownstone structure,

Cooper Union ❷, established by inventor and entrepreneur Peter Cooper in 1859 as a college for the underprivileged (it's still free of charge). Abraham Lincoln made his famous 'Might Makes Right' speech here in 1860, cementing his bid for the presidential nomination. The high-rise **Cooper Square Hotel** that appeared here recently is a very tangible sign of gentrification.

St Mark's Place

Turn around and head along the East Village's 'main street,' **St Mark's Place ❸**. The attitude here is a good-natured mix of punk, funk, and radical politics. Sidewalk cafés heave with customers, and the bazaar-like atmosphere is augmented by street vendors selling T-shirts, jewelry, and bootleg DVDs. Bars and restaurants are plentiful and filled with local characters; for years they have been hanging out one block south at **McSorley's Old Ale House**, see ⑪②.

Public Theater

From McSorley's turn right and cross Cooper Square. A few steps north on Fourth Avenue is **Astor Place ❹**, where there is a handsome cast-iron subway kiosk, as well as a black cube by Tony Rosenthal called *The Alamo*.

Walk south on Lafayette Street to the **Public Theater ❺**, headquartered in the majestic Astor Library, and built in the late 19th century. The theater is devoted to both Shakespeare and new plays, some of which have become major hits, like *Hair* and *A Chorus Line*.

Across the street, another architectural highlight, the 1831 **Colonnade Row**, houses the **Astor Place Theatre**, where the Blue Man Group is in residence.

Above from far left:
The Alamo by Tony Rosenthal on Astor Place; hanging out in Alphabet City; Veniero's Pasticceria; McSorley's Old Ale House.

Alphabet City

Just by Tompkins Square Park is Alphabet City, so named because of its avenues A, B, C, and D. Once known for crime and poverty, many of its slums have been replaced by restaurants and bars that attract a hip young crowd.

Food and Drink 🍴

① VENIERO'S PASTICCERIA

342 East 11th Street (near First Avenue); tel: 212-674-7070; Sun–Thur 8am–12am, Fri–Sat 8am–1am; $
A classic Italian pastry shop and café founded in 1894.

② MCSORLEY'S OLD ALE HOUSE

15 East 7th Street (near Third Avenue); tel: 212-474-9148; Mon–Sat 11am–1am, Sun 1pm–1am; $
In business since the 1850s, this classic New York saloon still has sawdust on the floors.

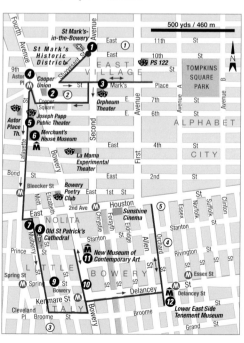

Above from left:
Little Italy; late 19th-century kitchen in the Lower East Side Tenement Museum.

Chinatown
One of Manhattan's most vibrant neighborhoods, and great for food, Chinatown started in the 1870s when Chinese railroad workers drifted east from California. The best place to learn about the neighborhood is the Museum of Chinese in the Americas, at 215 Centre Street.

Historic Interlude

If you're a history buff, turn left on East 4th Street for the **Merchant's House Museum ❻** (29 East 4th Street; tel: 212-777-1089; Thur–Mon noon–5pm; charge). Built in 1832, this Greek Revival townhouse was home to the Tredwell family until the 1930s. Several rooms and a 'secret' garden serve as a time capsule of upper-class life in the 19th and early 20th centuries.

NOLITA AND LITTLE ITALY

Continue four blocks south on Lafayette to East Houston Street. The area just south of Houston is a fun, savvy, boutique-laden lair known as **NoLita**. **Mulberry Street ❼** is the heart of this temple to trendy retail, and there are lots of watering holes and restaurants in the surrounding side streets.

Old St Patrick's Cathedral ❽ was the seat of the Catholic archdiocese until 1879, when the 'new' St Patrick's Cathedral on Fifth Avenue was completed. Services were held in Italian, highlighting the fact that this part of the city was in **Little Italy ❾**.

Although NoLita (**No**rth of **Li**ttle **Ita**ly) and **Chinatown** *(see margin, left)* farther south have both encroached upon its borders, Little Italy is still an atmospheric place for a meal, especially during the Feast of San Gennaro, the annual 10-day event which is held during the month of September. Head further down Mulberry Street to sample the atmosphere and the restaurants, such as **Da Nico**, see ❸.

LOWER EAST SIDE

The Lower East Side, which slants south of East Houston Street to the East River, is where Jewish immigrants from Eastern Europe settled toward the end of the 19th century. In and around the early 20th century, this was the most densely populated place in the world, with as many as 1,000 people per acre on its mean streets.

These days you'll see Chinese or Hispanic stores that, despite retaining Jewish names, demonstrate that the neighborhood still attracts new arrivals. Lately these have included trendy young New Yorkers, and with them, the advent of the fashionable boutiques, bars, and hotels that thrive around Orchard, Ludlow, and Rivington streets.

The Bowery

East of NoLita and Little Italy is the **Bowery ❿**, a long north–south street

---

Food and Drink

③ DA NICO
164 Mulberry Street; tel: 212-343-1212; daily L and D; $$
Old-style Little Italy restaurant where former mayor Rudolph Giuliani may be seen eating.

④ THE ORCHARD
162 Orchard Street; tel: 212-353-3570; daily B, L, and D; $
Cozy café with huge windows upstairs and creative fare. Handy before or after a trip to the adjacent Tenement Museum.

⑤ KATZ'S DELICATESSEN
205 East Houston Street (at Ludlow Street); tel: 212-254-2246; daily B, L, and D; $$
This Jewish deli is a New York institution, and the huge space is often filled to capacity. You might recognize it from the famous fake orgasm scene in the film *When Harry Met Sally*.

that gave this section of the Lower East Side its name. For years considered Manhattan's Skid Row, even this notoriously seedy strip is getting the Soho treatment, as posh nightclubs, designer shops, and million-dollar lofts open amid flophouses and whiskey joints.

Underscoring this gentrification is the **New Museum of Contemporary Art** ⑪ (No. 235 at Prince Street; www.newmuseum.org; Wed, Sun 11am–6pm, Thur until 9pm; charge) showing avant-garde work by living artists.

Tenement Museum

From the art museum head south two blocks and turn left onto Delancy Street. Five blocks along is Orchard Street where, on the corner at No. 108, you will find the visitor centre for the **Lower East Side Tenement Museum** ⑫ (tel: 212-431-0233; tours daily; charge). The museum is a thematic tour of an actual 1863 tenement building at No. 97. Over a span of seven decades this one building housed more than 7,000 people from some 20 countries. The building can only be seen by guided tour; these book up in advance and times vary, so call ahead or check the website for reservations. A limited number of same-day tickets are available at the visitor center. The museum also offers neighborhood walking tours.

Orchard Street to Houston

The best way to get further acquainted with this neighborhood is to walk up Orchard Street from the museum to Houston Street. If possible, visit on Sunday, when Orchard is at its busiest

(many stores are closed Friday afternoon and Saturday in observance of the Jewish Sabbath).

Once crowded with peddlers selling cut-rate clothing, **Orchard Street** today still offers some discount designer fashions, but the old shops are giving way to quirky boutiques and vintage clothes shops, some with tiny backroom art galleries. There are also several cool cafés in the neighbourhood, including **The Orchard**, see ⑪④. Another option is **Katz's Delicatessen**, see ⑪⑤, a great place to end this tour with a large meal.

Sunshine Theater
The latest indie films and popcorn in eight flavors draw movie-lovers to Sunshine Cinema, 143 East Houston Street, between First and Second avenues.

Traditional Eats

No tour of the Lower East Side is complete without visiting a few of the neighborhood's delis, bakeries, and candy shops. Tank up for a long day of walking at Yonah Schimmel Bakery (137 East Houston St), where knishes – mounds of dough stuffed with potato, spinach, or kasha – are baked in a brick oven. A few doors away, you can pick up paper-thin lox (smoked salmon), caviar, and herring at Russ & Daughters (179 E. Houston). At Essex and Rivington is the Essex Street Market, where vendors sell produce, meats, and more. Around the corner, Economy Candy (108 Rivington St) has been satisfying New York's sweet tooth since the 1930s, and Sugar Sweet Sunshine (126 Rivington St) turns out cakes and cupcakes.

If you're near the Tenement Museum, try ice cream and sorbet at Il Laboratorio del Gelato (95 Orchard St) or a salty, garlicky pickle at Guss' Pickles (85 Orchard St), trading since 1910. About three blocks away, Kossar's Bialys (367 Grand St) offers up bagels and warm, pliant bialys (onion rolls).

LOWER MANHATTAN

A tour of the Financial District, taking in the New York Stock Exchange, Federal Hall, Trinity Church, and the site of the World Trade Center, plus a walk along the Hudson River and a visit to the South Street Seaport.

DISTANCE 2¾ miles (4km)
TIME A full day
START Stock Exchange
END South Street Seaport
POINTS TO NOTE

While this tour could easily take a full day, you may wish to do the first half in the morning, including lunch at the World Financial Center, and then catch a ferry from Battery Park in the afternoon either to the Statue of Liberty and Ellis Island, or to Staten Island (tour 16).

Lower Manhattan is the original New York, where winding streets lead to busy, international docks. Today, these narrow byways are lined by towering temples of finance, museums, elegant churches, and, on the eastern side, South Street Seaport, a complex of historic waterfront buildings, ships, dining, and shops.

Start this tour in the heart of the Financial District: outside the imposing neoclassical temple that houses the **New York Stock Exchange ❶** on Broad Street just a few steps from Wall Street. Inside, the trading floor is a frenzy of yelling traders, flashing computers, and papers flying every which way; it's a roller coaster of buying and selling that, for better or worse, underpins the American economy.

Did You Know?
Wall Street was named after a wooden stockade erected by Dutch colonists to keep British neighbors at arm's length.

WALL STREET

For security reasons, the Exchange is no longer open to tourists, so walk instead to the corner of Wall Street and turn right for **Federal Hall ❷** (26 Wall Street; tel: 212-825-6990; Mon–Fri 9am–5pm, some Sats in summer; free), a Greek Revival edifice built in 1842 on what was the site of the British City Hall. George Washington was inaugurated as the country's first president here in 1789, an event commemorated by the statue at the top of the steps. Inside are free exhibits focusing on American history with an emphasis on the role of New York City and its many prominent residents.

Anyone keen on history may also want to investigate the **Museum of American Finance ❸** (48 Wall Street; tel: 212-908-4110; www.moac. org; Tue–Sat 10am–4pm; charge), housed in the former Bank of New York headquarters, near Federal Hall.

Trinity Church

Double back on Wall Street about three blocks to Broadway, where the Gothic bell tower of **Trinity Church ❹** rises up like an exclamation point. Surrounding the church are some of the city's oldest graves: Trinity's cemetery is a serene chronicle of three centuries of New York history. The

best known of the cemetery's residents is Alexander Hamilton, the first Secretary of the US Treasury, who was killed in a duel with political rival Aaron Burr in 1804.

Before moving on, poke your head into the lobby of the handsome **Bank of New York** ❺ (formerly the Irving Trust Co.) back across Broadway at 1 Wall Street. This is an Art Deco treasure with a rippling gray facade and brilliant red-and-gold mosaics.

WORLD TRADE CENTER SITE

Walk north on Broadway, then left on Liberty Street for a visit to the **Tribute WTC Visitor Center** ❻ (tel: 866-737-1184; www.tributewtc.org; Mon and Wed–Sat 10am–6pm, Tue noon–6pm, Sun noon–5pm; suggested donation), part of the **World Trade Center Site**. This non-profit organization was set up in the aftermath of the September 11, 2001 tragedy to allow those most

Above from far left: view of Lower Manhattan; banker on Wall Street; Pier 17 at South Street Seaport; New York Stock Exchange.

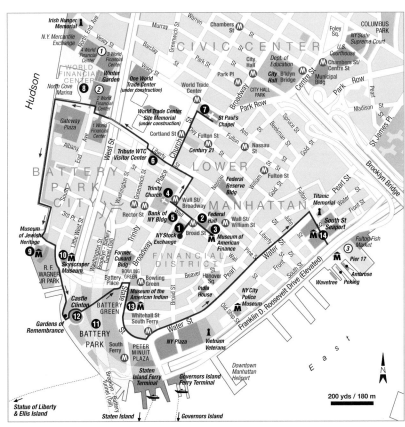

President's Pew
George Washington attended St Paul's Chapel during his brief residency in New York after his inauguration. The pew where he worshiped remains in the church.

affected to stay in touch. The center consists of five galleries. A documentary on life before the attack has testimonies from former employees and local residents, while other galleries focus on events as they unfold, and the rescue and clean-up operation. A visit to this moving memorial can be completed by taking a tour of the rest of the site, where the **One World Trade Center** tower is under construction, led by a volunteer of the September 11th community.

You'll find another contemplative experience by walking two blocks north on Church Street, then one block east on Fulton Street to **St Paul's Chapel** ❼ (209 Broadway), the city's oldest church, built in 1766. More modest than Trinity Church, St Paul's reflects the earlier Georgian style, and it too has a peaceful graveyard. A sanctuary in the difficult days after September 11th, the church houses a memorial exhibit.

WORLD FINANCIAL CENTER

Return to Liberty Street and continue west toward the Hudson River. A pedestrian bridge veers to the left and leads over the highway into the **World Financial Center** ❽. Here, a few shops and restaurants are clustered in a mall-like setting around the **Winter Garden**, a marble plaza with palm trees under a vaulted glass roof. If you're lucky, you might catch a lunchtime concert. Otherwise, take the opportunity to eat at **Au Mandarin**, see ❶①, or stock up on energy to continue the rest of the tour at the **Elixir Juice Bar**, see ❶②.

Below: *An Icon of Hope* in Battery Park.

HUDSON RIVER ESPLANADE

It's about a 10-minute walk south along the river **Esplanade** to the **Museum of Jewish Heritage** ❾ (36 Battery Place; tel: 646-437-4200; www.mjhnyc.org; Sun–Thur 10am–5.45pm, Wed until 8pm, Fri 10am–3pm; charge). The museum opened by the spot where Jews first set foot in North America in 1654. Exhibits draw from a rich pool of personal artifacts to present the story of the Jewish people and put the Holocaust into the context of 20th-century history.

Across Battery Place, the intriguing **Skyscraper Museum** ❿ (39 Battery Place; tel: 212-968-1961; www.skyscraper.org; Wed–Sun noon–6pm; charge) explores the history and technology of high-rise buildings.

Battery Park

Follow Battery Place to **Battery Park** ⓫ at Manhattan's southern tip. Encompassed within its 21 acres (8 hectares) are gardens, walkways, and monuments, including a spherical bronze sculpture that was salvaged from the rubble of the World Trade Center Plaza and reinstalled here as a 9/11 memorial. It's called *An Icon of Hope*.

At the water's edge is **Castle Clinton** ⓬ (daily 8.30am–5pm; free), a stone fort built as a defense against the British during the run-up to the War of 1812 and later used as a theater, immigration station, and aquarium. Today, it holds a small museum and serves as the ticket office for the **Statue of Liberty and Ellis Island ferries** *(see p.94)*.

Museum of the American Indian

Across State Street from Battery Park is the **National Museum of the American Indian** ⑬ (1 Bowling Green, tel: 212-514-3700; www.nmai.si.edu; daily 10am–5pm, Thur until 8pm; free), housed in the ornate Beaux Arts Custom House designed by Cass Gilbert in the early 1900s. The museum showcases highlights from a vast collection of Native American art held by the Smithsonian Institution.

Bowling Green

The museum fronts a cobbled plaza known as **Bowling Green**, New York's oldest public park and site of the massive 7,000lb (3,000kg) bronze *Charging Bull*, created in 1989 by Arturo Di Modica. In an act of unrestrained (and unauthorized) generosity, the sculptor installed the piece outside the New York Stock Exchange as a gift to the people of New York. After a bit of legal wrangling, the city had it moved here. It is commonly believed among stockbrokers that rubbing a certain part of the bull's anatomy brings good luck to the market.

SOUTH STREET SEAPORT

From Bowling Green, State Street loops around past Whitehall Street and the **Staten Island Ferry Terminal** *(see p.95)* to Water Street, where you can either hail a cab, hop on a bus, or walk about 10 blocks to Fulton Street, then right to the **South Street Seaport** ⑭ (12–14 Fulton Street; tel: 212-748-8600; www. southstreetseaport.com; Mon–Sat 10am–9pm, Sun 11am–8pm; free).

Not a museum in the conventional sense, the seaport is an 11-block historic district on the East River that combines shops, restaurants, vintage ships, and nautical exhibitions. In the mid-1800s this was the country's busiest port, but the advent of large steamships shifted sea traffic to the deeper waters of the Hudson River.

Old ships at Piers 15 and 16 are the chief historic attraction. Nearby is the **Pier 17 Pavilion**, with stores, cafés, and a food court offering vistas of the **Brooklyn Bridge**. Also nearby is **Schermerhorn Row**, built 1810–12 to house maritime offices and warehouses and which now functions as gallery space for changing exhibits.

There are quite a few snack bars and other casual eating places at the seaport, but for the best views, it's hard to go wrong at **Harbour Lights**, see ⑪③.

Above from far left: the Winter Garden in the World Financial Center; the *Peking*, a four-masted sailing barque, at the South Street Seaport.

Patriotic Fervor
Worked into a frenzy by a reading of the *Declaration of Independence*, a mob in 1776 tore down a statue of King George III in Bowling Green and melted it down into musket balls, supposedly shot at British troops.

Food and Drink

① AU MANDARIN
World Financial Center, 200–250 Vesey Street; tel: 212-385-0313; daily L and D; $$
The fare at this upscale Chinese restaurant is a cut above the usual takeout joint. A popular lunch spot for traders, it's a good choice for a quick, tasty sit-down meal.

② ELIXIR JUICE BAR
Two World Financial Center, 225 Liberty Street; tel: 212-945-0400; daily 7am–7pm; $
The smoothies at this takeout place are practically a meal in themselves, and, according to the owners, can help cure a wide variety of afflictions, from bad breath to arthritis.

③ HARBOUR LIGHTS
South Street Seaport, Pier 17, 3rd floor; tel: 212-227-2800; daily L and D, Sat–Sun Br; $$
A spectacular view of the Brooklyn Bridge makes good surf 'n' turf taste even better.

STATUE OF LIBERTY AND ELLIS ISLAND

Stop for coffee and pastries near Wall Street, then board the ferry to the monumental statue and historic building that received more than 12 million new arrivals during the great age of American immigration.

Thin-Skinned
The Statue of Liberty's copper skin is hammered to less than an eighth of an inch (3mm) thick but weighs more than 90 tons.

Governors Island
Once a major US military base, this is now 172 acres (70 hectares) of parkland offering walking and biking trails, historic forts and buildings, picnicking and peerless views. Free 10-minute ferry rides from the Maritime Terminal near Battery Park Fri 10am–5pm, Sat–Sun 10am–7pm June–October (www. govisland.com).

DISTANCE 3 miles (5km)
TIME A half-day
START Stone Street
END Battery Park
POINTS TO NOTE

Ferries to the Statue of Liberty and Ellis Island depart from Battery Park in Lower Manhattan every 20 to 30 minutes from approx. 9.30am to 6pm (seasonal variations). Tickets can be bought at Castle Clinton.

Free park-ranger-led tours of both islands are conducted daily. To tour the Statue of Liberty itself a time-pass is required; these are available on a first-come, first-served basis at Castle Clinton, but it is far safer to reserve ahead by phone (877-523-9849) or online at www.statuecruises.com.

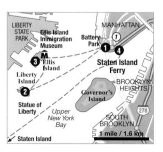

This tour's first port of call is **Financier Patisserie**, see ⑪①, on **Stone Street**, for coffee and pastries to set you up for the day. Once sated, head south to **Battery Park ❶**, for the ferry to the Statue of Liberty.

STATUE OF LIBERTY

The **Statue of Liberty ❷** (Liberty Island; www.nps.gov/stli; tel: 212-363-3200; ferries daily approx. 9.30am–5pm; charge for ferry, statue free, *see box, left*), or to give her full name, *Liberty Enlightening the World*, was a gift from the people of France, and was conceived by Edouard-René Lefebvre de Laboulaye, a Gallic admirer of American democracy.

De Laboulaye conveyed his enthusiasm to sculptor Frédéric-Auguste Bartholdi, who not only designed the monument but took a leading role in raising funds for its construction. The engineer Gustave Eiffel, who would later gain enduring renown for his eponymous tower erected for the 1889 World Fair, designed the trusswork that supports the copper skin.

The statue was completed in France in July 1884, and arrived in New York Harbor in June 1885 on

board the French frigate *Isère*. In transit, Lady Liberty and her crown, torch, tablet, and other accessories were reduced to 350 pieces and packed in 214 crates. It took four months to reassemble the statue in its entirety. On October 28 1886, a dedication by President Grover Cleveland took place in front of thousands of spectators.

ELLIS ISLAND

After visiting the statue, the ferry continues to **Ellis Island ❸**, which was for 62 years, from 1892 to 1954, the gateway to the United States, and known as the 'Island of Tears,' because of the stress caused to applicants by the strict medical, mental, and literacy tests imposed. Today, more than 100 million Americans are descendants of the around 12 million immigrants who landed at Ellis Island in search of a better life.

Immigration Museum
Allowed to fall into ruin after it was closed in 1954, the main building on the island was restored with $156 million in private funds, and in 1990 reopened as the **Ellis Island Immigration Museum** (tel: 212-363-3200; www.ellisisland.org; ferries as for Statue of Liberty; charge for ferry), chronicling the island's history. Exhibits are arranged on three floors and include photographs, artifacts, personal papers, and audio recordings to recreate the process of entering the country.

After a tour, take time to enjoy the views of the Manhattan skyline from the promenade, before catching a ferry back to the mainland.

STATEN ISLAND FERRY

The **Staten Island Ferry ❹** may be the best tourist deal in New York. The free, 20-minute ferry shuttles passengers between the Whitehall Terminal adjacent to Battery Park and St George Terminal on Staten Island. Views of the Statue of Liberty and Lower Manhattan are excellent. The panorama is especially inspiring after dark.

Above from far left: the American Immigrant Wall of Honor on Ellis Island; Lady Liberty; photos of immigrants at the Ellis Island Immigration Museum; the museum viewed from the ferry.

Below: the Staten Island Ferry offers superb views – free of charge.

Food and Drink

① FINANCIER PATISSERIE

62 Stone Street (at Mill Lane); tel: 212-344-5600; Mon–Sat B and L; $

Start the day with coffee and a choice of tarts, croissants, and other pastries at this delightful café on a cobbled side street closed to traffic. Lunch is nice, too, with soups, salads, and hot-press sandwiches. Outdoor tables shaded with umbrellas give the patisserie an authentic Parisian feel.

BROOKLYN

Catch a subway train to the suburbs and unwind with the Brooklynites in Prospect Park, which is home to Brooklyn Botanic Garden and the wonderfully eclectic Brooklyn Museum of Art.

Coney Island

At the southern tip of Brooklyn, Coney Island has been entertaining New Yorkers since the 1860s. There are amusement rides, the beach, and Nathan's Famous hot dogs.

DISTANCE 1½ miles (2.5km)
TIME A half- to full day
START/END Grand Army Plaza
POINTS TO NOTE

This tour focuses on the Prospect Park area of Brooklyn. To get to the starting point take the 2 or 3 train to Grand Army Plaza. If you want to spend a longer amount of time in Brooklyn, consider a scenic walk across the Brooklyn Bridge and/or a visit to one of the borough's many neighborhoods, such as Brooklyn Heights or DUMBO.

Food and Drink

① ROSE WATER

787 Union Street; tel: 718-783 3800; daily D, Sat–Sun Br (10am–3pm); $$–$$$

With a dinky dining room and sheltered terrace, Rose Water does seasonal American food, with the focus on quality organic ingredients. The weekend *prix-fixe* brunch menu of fluffy eggs, waffles, and spongy French toast is popular with laidback locals.

② APPLEWOOD

501 11th Street; tel: 718-788-1810; Tue–Sat D, Sun Br; $$–$$$

With a lovely leafy terrace, this unpretentious restaurant serves outstanding food, with the emphasis on seasonal, ethically sourced, local ingredients. It's an excellent choice for a meal (from 5pm) at the end of a day in Brooklyn, or Sunday brunch. Start with warm home-baked bread, continue with delicate Chatham cod or juicy, flavorful roast organic chicken, then finish with beautifully presented classics such as chocolate soufflé.

Brooklyn is the city's most populated borough, connected to Lower Manhattan by the striking **Brooklyn Bridge**. Opened in 1883 and called the 'eighth wonder of the world,' the construction of the steel-cable suspension bridge was a challenge and a marvel, despite being marred by tragedy (12 people were killed on its opening day).

Brooklyn has many neighborhoods, some dating from the borough's days of Dutch occupancy in the 1600s. One area that is always desirable is **Brooklyn Heights**; the **Brooklyn Heights Promenade** has handsome townhouses on one side and views of Manhattan and the East River on the other.

When Soho became too expensive, artists moved over the water to lofts in **DUMBO** (**D**own **U**nder the **M**anhattan **B**ridge **O**verpass), then to **Williamsburg** and **Red Hook**. Any of these areas is worth an afternoon's visit, strolling around the galleries and shops.

Since Brooklyn is so large, this tour concentrates on the attractions in the Prospect Park area.

PROSPECT PARK

Start at **Grand Army Plaza ❶**, a monumental square with a triumphal arch that serves as the entrance to 585-acre (237-hectare) **Prospect Park**.

The park was designed in 1866 by Frederick Law Olmsted and Calvert Vaux and is thought by many to exceed their achievement in Central Park *(see p.46)*, which they designed eight years earlier. A short walk leads into **Long Meadow ❷**, a mile of gently sloping grassland where Brooklynites come to picnic, play ball, and generally unwind.

BOTANIC GARDEN

Return to Grand Army Plaza and a short walk east on Eastern Parkway leads to the **Brooklyn Botanic Garden ❸** (tel: 718-623-7200; www.bbg.org; Tue–Fri 8am–4.30pm, Sat–Sun 10am–4.30pm, extended summer hours; charge), which is made up of 52 acres (21 hectares) of specialty gardens, with a program of concerts and festivals.

BROOKLYN MUSEUM OF ART

Also accessible from Eastern Parkway is the **Brooklyn Museum of Art ❹** (tel: 718-638-5000; www.brooklynmuseum. org; Wed–Fri 10am–5pm, Sat–Sun 11am–6pm; charge), second only to the Metropolitan as New York City's largest. There are 28 period rooms and an unusual outdoor sculpture garden. Scholars and art fans from all over the world come here to study the museum's respected Egyptian collection.

Every first Saturday of the month, Brooklyn Museum extends its opening hours until 11pm. With free admission, music and dance shows in the lobby, and wine served in the late-closing Museum Café, there's quite a buzz.

EATING OUT

The Museum and Botanic Garden have cafés, and there are some great dinner and brunch options nearby. For **Rose Water**, see ⑪①, return to Grand Army Plaza and take Union Street three blocks northwest; for **Applewood**, see ⑪②, take 11th Street northwest from the western edge of Prospect Park.

Above from far left: the Brooklyn Bridge; DUMBO is an area popular with artists; *George Washington* by Gilbert Scott in the Brooklyn Museum of Art; the Cherry Esplanade in the Botanic Garden.

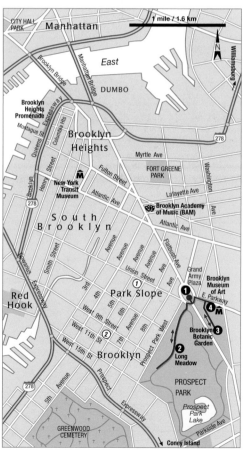

THE BRONX

Take a day trip to the Bronx for a stroll through one of the world's premier botanical centers, a tour of the country's largest urban zoo, and dinner in New York's 'other' Little Italy.

Pelham Bay Park and City Island
On the Bronx's eastern shore, where the East River meets Long Island Sound, is Pelham Bay Park, the largest in New York City. A bridge leads from the park to City Island, a seaside community reminiscent of a New England village.

DISTANCE 3 miles (5km)
TIME A half- to full day
START Botanical Garden Station
END Fordham Road Station
POINTS TO NOTE

To get to the Botanical Garden take the Metro–North Harlem local line from Grand Central Terminal to Botanical Garden Station. The journey takes 20 minutes (tel: 212-532-4900 or www.mta.info for schedules). To return to Grand Central from Arthur Avenue, walk to – or catch a cab to – Fordham Road Station (417 East Fordham Road at Third Avenue). Bear in mind that the garden is closed Mondays, and that selected zoo attractions are closed in winter when some animals hibernate.

Food and Drink 🍴

① **DOMINICK'S**
2335 Arthur Avenue (at 187th Street); tel: 718-733-2807; daily L and D; $$
Fans of Dominick's claim that this is the real Little Italy. There's no menu; the waiter tells you all you need to know. There's no check at the end: they just size you up and pronounce a figure.

② **ROBERTO'S**
632 Crescent Avenue (at 186th Street); tel: 718-733-9503; Tue–Fri L and D, Sat–Sun D; $$
Roberto will pop out of the kitchen in his whites to meet and greet, while his floury-handed mama may say hello in between preparing batches of pasta. A true slice of Italian life.

In 1641 a Scandinavian, Jonas Bronck, bought 500 acres (200 hectares) of the New World from Native Americans. After building his home on virgin land, he and his family found the area remote and lonely, so they threw parties for friends. The Indian land was called Keskeskeck (or Rananchqua, the native Siwanou name), but the name was changed, the story goes, by Manhattanites asking their friends, 'Where are you going on Saturday night?' and being answered, 'Why, to the Broncks'.'

The validity of the anecdote is questionable, but the area had been virgin forest, and it did begin with Jonas's farm. Part of its original hemlock forest remains in Bronx Park, which includes the zoo as well as the 250-acre (100-hectare) New York Botanical Garden, where this tour begins.

BOTANICAL GARDEN

From the Botanical Garden station walk across Kazimiroff Boulevard to the Mosholu Gate of the **New York Botanical Garden** ❶ (tel: 718-817-8700; Apr–Oct Tue–Sun 10am–6pm, Nov–Mar Tue–Sun 10am–5pm; charge). More than 40 specialty gardens offer welcome sanctuary from the frenetic pace of city life; the garden is especially attractive in spring when its cherry trees,

magnolias, daffodils, and tulips are in full bloom. The **Enid A. Haupt Conservatory** is a highlight, a crystal palace with a Palm Court and greenhouses constructed in 1902. The **Rockefeller Rose Garden** is a vision not to be missed in late May–early June, and the **Everett Children's Adventure Garden** has pint-size topiaries and mazes that make for hours of fun for youngsters.

BRONX ZOO

Next stop is the **Bronx Zoo ②** (Bronx River Parkway and Fordham Road; tel: 718-220-5100; www.bronxzoo.com; Apr–Oct Mon–Fri 10am–5pm, Sat–Sun 10am–5.30pm, Nov–Mar daily 10am–4.30pm; charge), a20-minute walk away. To get here, exit the Botanical Garden from Conservatory Gate, turn left down Kazimiroff Boulevard, cross Fordham Road and continue along Southern Boulevard until you reach the pedestrian entrance on your left.

This is the largest metropolitan zoo in the United States and home to around 4,500 animals, including endangered species. The attractions include a monorail ride over **Wild Asia** (home to Asian elephants, rhinoceros, and antelopes), a 40-acre (16-hectare) complex with moats to keep the big cats away from their prey (ie the spectators), and the **Congo Gorilla Forest**, 6½ acres (2.5 hectares) of forest and bamboo thickets that are home to around 20 lowland gorillas. There's also a sea-lion pool, bison range, butterfly garden, and children's zoo, as well as indoor facilities for nocturnal animals, reptiles, monkeys, and more.

LITTLE ITALY

Take a cab to end your tour with an Italian meal at **Dominick's**, see ⑪①, in the **Belmont** neighborhood, the Bronx's Little Italy, around **Arthur Avenue ③** and East 187th Street (which joins the Southern Boulevard). Another good choice is **Roberto's**, see ⑪②. When it's time to leave, catch a cab to Fordham Road station, especially if it is getting dark; you should take extra care in this neighborhood.

Above from far left: Bronx Zoo; New York Botanical Garden; Belmont is the Little Italy of the Bronx; head to Arthur Avenue for an Italian meal.

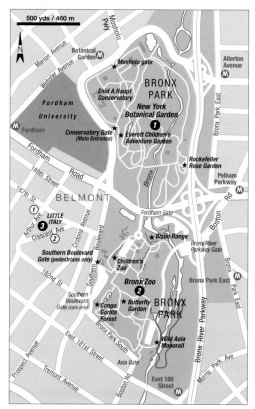

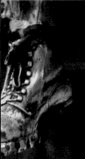

DIRECTORY

A user-friendly alphabetical listing of practical information, plus hand-picked hotels and restaurants, clearly organized by area, to suit all budgets and tastes.

A

AIRPORTS AND ARRIVALS

New York's major international airports are John F. Kennedy and Liberty International in nearby New Jersey. Allow an hour's driving time for each, more during rush hours. LaGuardia, serving domestic flights only, is a 30-minute drive.

AirTrain is a subway-to-rail connection between JFK and the city (tel: 877-535-2478; www.airtrainjfk.com), or there is a train from Penn Station to Newark Airport (tel: 888-EWR-INFO; www.airtrainnewark.com). New York Airport Service (tel: 212-875-8200; www.nyairportservice.com) operates buses to and from LaGuardia and JFK from the Port Authority Bus Terminal, Penn Station, Grand Central Terminal, and some Midtown hotels. Olympia

Trails (tel: 877-8-NEWARK; www.CoachUSA.com/Olympia) runs express buses between Newark Airport and the Port Authority Bus Terminal, Penn Station, and Grand Central Terminal.

Door-to-door minibus service between Manhattan and all airports is provided by Super Shuttle (tel: 800-258-3826; www.supershuttle.com) and AirLink (tel: 212-812-9000; www.goairlinkshuttle.com). Prices are attractive, but allow an extra two hours for additional passenger pickups on the way.

Taxis to Midtown run $25–30 from LaGuardia, fixed price $45 from JFK, about $50 from Newark, plus tolls. Many travelers use private limo services such as Carmel (tel: 212-666-6666; www.carmel), with rates only slightly more than taxicabs.

C

CLIMATE AND CLOTHES

New York City has four distinct seasons (see Climate, p.12). Average annual rainfall is 44in (112cm); raincoats and umbrellas are a good idea year-round.

Dress tends to be casual, but it is advisable to ask about proper dress for restaurants, nightclubs, etc.

CRIME AND SAFETY

Despite its recent reputation as a 'caring, sharing New York,' parts of the city can hold hazards, and visitors should not be lulled into a false sense of security. Adopt the typical New Yorker's guise of looking street-smart

---

Children

Preparation – and lots of patience – are the keys to a successful trip with children. In some respects, New York is the perfect family destination because there are so many activities that both adults and children will enjoy: a Broadway show, for example, or a trip to the Central Park Zoo. For kids who aren't accustomed to big-city life, even mundane experiences will be an adventure. You may be smitten by the city's art and culture, but what your kids may remember most is riding the subway, a playground or bike ride through Central Park, or buying hot dogs from a street vendor.

and aware at all times and avoid ostentatious displays of jewelry or wealth that invite muggers. Excursions into deserted areas at night (such as Central Park or Battery Park) are equally unwise. Lock your hotel door even when you are inside, and travel to neighborhoods like Harlem in a group. Although Times Square has thrown off its seedy reputation, the crowded streets around this area attract pickpockets, so keep wallets in a secure place.

Although the subways are much safer than they were, people traveling alone late at night should stay on alert. Once through the turnstile, stay within sight of the ticket booth and try to get on a carriage where there are other people.

CUSTOMS REGULATIONS

For information on US Customs regulations, go to www.customs.ustreas.gov.

D

DISABLED TRAVELERS

All city buses and a few major subway stops are accessible, as are most restaurants. Disabled travelers can obtain information about rights and special facilities from the Mayor's Office for People with Disabilities (tel: 212-788-2830; www.nyc.gov/mopd).

DRIVING IN NEW YORK

Driving is the least efficient way to get around. Drivers are aggressive, traffic is frequently snarled, street parking is scant

(and tickets are punitive), and commercial parking is extremely expensive.

If a car is needed, rentals are available at airports and all over the city. You must be at least 21 to rent a car, have a valid driver's license, and a major credit card. Be sure you are insured for both collision and personal liability.

E

ELECTRICITY

Standard American electric current is 110 volts. An adapter is necessary for European appliances, which run on 220–240 volts.

EMBASSIES AND CONSULATES

Australia Mission to the UN: 150 East 42nd Street; tel: 212-351-6600.
British Consulate-General: 845 Third Avenue; tel: 212-745-0200.
Canadian Consulate-General: 1251 Sixth Avenue; tel: 212-596-1783.
Consulate General of Ireland: 345 Park Avenue; tel: 212-319-2555.
New Zealand Mission to the UN: 1 UN Plaza; tel: 212-826-1960.
Consulate of South Africa: 333 East 38th Street; tel: 212-213-4880.

EMERGENCY NUMBERS

Police, fire, ambulance: tel: 911.
Referral service: tel: 311.
Dental emergency: tel: 212-486-9458.
Health emergency: tel: 212-737-1212.
Report Sex Crimes: tel: 212-267-7273.

Above from far left: Uptown view from the Empire State Building; a sunny day in Central Park.

Drinking Age
The legal drinking age in New York is 21. Be prepared to show picture identification before purchasing alcohol or entering a bar. Some nightclubs admit under-21 patrons but card everyone who attempts to buy a drink.

Above from left:
dog owners are
expected to clean
up after their pets;
Bloomingdale's
signature 'brown
bag'; NYPD
motorcycle cop;
richly embellished
Rockefeller Center.

ENTRY REGULATIONS

Information on US entry regulations is found at http://travel.state.gov.

ETIQUETTE

New Yorkers have a reputation for being brusque and outspoken. It's a generalization, but not entirely unfounded. This is a fast-paced city with a hard-charging attitude. That said, you will find that most citizens are very helpful if you seek assistance. This is also an extraordinarily diverse city. And while New Yorkers are hardly paragons of universal brotherhood, they manage to get along in a sort of workaday fashion that keeps the city from flying apart at the seams.

GAY AND LESBIAN

The traditional epicenter of New York's large gay community used to be Greenwich Village – the West Village in particular, on and around Christopher Street – but recently the center of gravity has shifted to Chelsea. Other popular neighborhoods are the East Village and Hell's Kitchen, in the 40s, west of the Theater District. Gay and lesbian travelers will find Manhattan a mostly tolerant and friendly place with a host of bars and clubs where gays congregate. Gay Pride Week in late June is celebrated with a big Fifth Avenue parade, and the annual flamboyant Halloween Parade in Greenwich Village brings thousands of spectators.

Useful Resources

Lesbian, Gay, Bisexual and Transgender Community Center: 208 West 13th Street (at Seventh Avenue); tel: 212-620-7310; www.gaycenter.org; daily 9am–11pm. This large and helpful organization offers services and events ranging from health education, counseling, and political action to parties.

Gay and Lesbian Hotline: tel: 212-989-0999; Mon–Fri 4pm–midnight, Sat noon–5pm. Provides information about all aspects of gay life in New York, from bars to legal counseling.

Gay & Lesbian Anti-Violence Project: 240 West 35th Street; tel: 212-714-1184; www.avp.org. Organization providing legal advocacy for victims of anti-gay violence.

Gay Men's Health Crisis: 119 West 24th Street; tel: 212-367-1000; www.gmhc.org. This non-profit group assists people with HIV/AIDS.

Newspapers and Magazines

Gay City News: gaycitynews.com. Covers local, national, and world news. **Next**: www.nextmagazine.net. Dedicated to entertainment in gay New York. **Time Out New York Magazine**: www. newyork.timeout.com. Runs a large weekly listing of gay clubs and events.

HEALTH AND MEDICAL CARE

Medical services are extremely expensive. Purchase comprehensive travel insurance to cover any emergencies.

Dogs
If you're traveling with a dog, keep in mind that it must be leashed in public places, and droppings must be cleaned up and disposed of properly. Scoopers are sold at pet shops and hardware stores, but many dog owners find it easier to use a plastic bag.

Two sources if you need non-emergency house calls are: Doctors on Call: tel: 718-238-2100; House Call Express: tel: 212-203-4869.

Emergency Medical Treatment

Bellevue Hospital: First Avenue and East 27th Street; tel: 212-562-4141.
Beth Israel Medical Center: First Avenue at 16th St; tel: 212-420-2840.
Lenox Hill Hospital: 77th Street and Park Avenue; tel: 212-434-2000.
Mount Sinai Hospital: Fifth Avenue and 100th Street; tel: 212-241-6500.
New York Presbyterian Hospital: 525 East 68th Street; tel: 212-746-5454.
New York Presbyterian Medical Center at Columbia University: 622 West 168th Street; tel: 212-305-2500.
NYU Medical Center: 550 First Avenue at 33rd Street; tel: 212-263-7300.
St Luke's-Roosevelt Hospital: 59th Street between Ninth and Tenth avenues; tel: 212-523-6800.

HOURS AND HOLIDAYS

Business Hours

Department stores and shops tend to stay open later, typically 10am to 8.30pm. Sunday hours are shorter, usually 11am to 6 or 7pm. Banks are normally open 9am to 3pm (although ATM machines are everywhere), but increasingly they are opening as early as 8am and staying open until late afternoon or early evening.

Public Holidays

The US has shifted most public holidays to the Monday closest to the actual dates, thereby creating a number of three-day weekends. Holidays that are observed no matter the day on which they fall are:
New Year's Day (January 1).
Independence Day (July 4).
Veterans' Day (November 11).
Christmas Day (December 25).

Other holidays are:
Martin Luther King Jr Day (third Mon in Jan).
President's Day (third Mon in Feb).
Memorial Day (last Mon in May).
Labor Day (first Mon in Sep).
Columbus Day (second Mon in Oct).
Election Day (first Tue in Nov).
Thanksgiving (fourth Thur in Nov).

L

LOST PROPERTY

The chances of retrieving lost property are not high, but the occasional civic-minded individual may turn items in to the nearest police precinct. To inquire about items left on public transportation (subway and bus), tel: 212-712-4500; Mon, Tue, Fri 8am–3.30pm, Wed, Thur 11am–6.30pm. Or call 311.

MAPS

NYC & Co. has good maps at their visitor center and online at www.nycgo.com. Subway and bus maps are available at subway station booths, or from the New York City Transit Authority booth

Internet
Free public WiFi (wireless internet access) is available in Union Square, Bryant Park, Chelsea Market, South Street Seaport, the Winter Garden (World Financial Center), Lincoln Center Park, public libraries throughout Manhattan, and in numerous cafés and restaurants. Most hotels are gearing up to provide WiFi in their guest rooms, too. Email can be sent from most branches of FedEx/Kinko's copy shops or from computers at most public libraries.

Above from left: the Stars and Stripes; the New York Public Library at Fifth Avenue and 42nd Street has free WiFi service.

Rest Stops When energy flags, New York has thoughtfully provided seating areas on Broadway between 42nd and 47th streets, at Herald Square between 33rd and 35th streets, and around Lincoln Center. Public restrooms are found in public parks but otherwise are in short supply in New York. Look for department stores, hotels, large book stores, or Starbucks coffee shops, which do have restrooms. In some cases you will have to request a key.

in Grand Central Terminal and the Long Island Rail Road information booth in Penn Station, as well as the MTA booth at the Times Square Visitors Center. You can also download them from www.mta.info.

MEDIA

Print

The *New York Times* and *Wall Street Journal* are both regarded as papers of national significance, and they are also strong on local issues. The *Times'* bulky Sunday edition has extensive coverage of local arts and entertainment.

Two papers compete for the tabloid market: the *New York Post* and the *Daily News*. There are two 'commuter' dailies distributed free in the mornings: *AM New York* and *Metro*. The free alternative weekly *Village Voice* has comprehensive listings and classified ads, as does the *New York Observer* and *New York Press*. Local magazines with extensive event listings include *New York* and *Time Out New York*.

Radio

There are more than 70 radio stations in New York City. Some of the better stations with local news include:

WNYC	93.9FM/820AM
WABC	770AM
WCBS	880AM
WINS	1010AM
WBBR	1130AM

Television

The three major networks – all with New York headquarters – are ABC

(Channel 7, 77 West 66th Street; tel: 212-456-7777), CBS (Channel 2, 51 West 52nd Street; tel: 212-975-4321), and NBC (Channel 4, 30 Rockefeller Plaza; tel: 212-664-4444). Fox News has a national office at 1211 Sixth Avenue (tel: 212-556-2500) and a local studio (Channel 5, 205 East 67th Street; tel: 212-452-3983). CNN has offices at the Time Warner Center. Channel 13, the local Public Broadcasting Service (PBS) affiliate, has open studios at Lincoln Center. The other local stations are UPN (9) and CW (11).

Various cable companies offer 50 or more specialized cable and movie channels. Check newspaper listings for channel numbers.

MONEY

Credit Cards and ATMs

Cash advances on major credit and debit cards can be obtained from bank tellers and bank ATMs (automatic teller machines), which are marked with the corresponding stickers (ie Cirrus, Plus, Visa, MasterCard, American Express, etc.) Most of these charge a fee for withdrawing cash. Credit cards are accepted almost everywhere, although not all cards at all places.

Currency Exchange

There are many outlets for exchanging currency and cashing travelers checks. These are accepted in most hotels and restaurants (as long as they are in dollars) and can be cashed at most banks. Some banks charge a fee for this service. Photo identification is required.

Travelex, a well-known source for currency exchange, has two convenient Midtown locations, tel: 800-287-7362; 1578 Broadway at 47th Street, tel: 212-265-6063; 1271 Broadway at 32nd Street, tel: 212-679-4365; and two Downtown offices, 29 Broadway, tel: 212-363-6206; and 30 Vesey Street, tel: 212-227-8156.

American Express has numerous offices around town for selling and cashing travelers checks, including 374 Park Avenue, tel: 212-421-8240; 151 West 34th Street, tel: 212-695-8075; and Marriott Marquis Hotel, 1535 Broadway, tel: 212-575-6580.

There is also an automated self-change kiosk at the Times Square Information Center at 1560 Broadway (between 46th and 47th streets).

Citibank offers exchange facilities at most branches. Tel: 800-285-3000.

Refunds

Department stores usually allow you to return merchandise up to 30 days after purchase for full credit. Boutiques are less accommodating; some allow store credit only, no returns on sale items, and no returns or exchanges after seven days.

POSTAL SERVICES

Manhattan's main post office is on Eighth Avenue between 31st and 33rd streets; it is open 24 hours a day. To locate post offices elsewhere in the five boroughs, call 800-275-8777 or go to www.usps.com.

RELIGION

New York is approximately 70 percent Christian, 11 percent Jewish, 1.5 percent Muslim, and 7.4 percent agnostic, with Buddhists, Hindus, and others also represented. Some 6,000 churches, synagogues, temples, and mosques can be found in the city's five boroughs.

TAXIS

Taxis, all metered, cruise the streets and must be hailed, although there are designated taxi stands at bus and train stations. Be sure to flag down an official yellow cab. The light on top is lit when the cab is available. The base rate on taxi fares is $3 upon entry plus 40¢ for every one-fifth of a mile (when the taxicab is traveling at 6 miles an hour or more) or 60 seconds (when not in motion). The flat rate for a taxi between JFK and Manhattan is $45 plus tolls. There is a $1 surcharge on all taxi rides from 4pm to 8pm on weekdays, and a 50¢ surcharge from 8pm to 6am.

24-hr taxi hotline: tel: 212-NYC-TAXI (212-692-8294).

Water Taxis

New York Water Taxis provide ferry service on the Hudson and East rivers. In addition to commuter services, water taxis offer hop-on-hop-off tours around the harbor on summer weekends and scenic tours. See www.nywatertaxi.com.

Smoking
There is currently a no-smoking law in effect in virtually all New York City bars, restaurants, and offices. Be sure to request a smoking room if needed when booking a place to stay. The legal age to buy cigarettes is 18.

Street Grid
In Midtown and Uptown Manhattan, avenues run north and south; streets run east and west. Even-numbered streets tend to have one-way eastbound traffic; odd-numbered streets, westbound traffic. Exceptions are 14th, 23rd, 57th, 72nd, 79th and 86th streets, which have two-way traffic and crosstown bus services. Most avenues are one-way, except for Park Avenue which has two-way traffic north of 44th Street, and Broadway north of 57th Street. The picture is more confusing in Greenwich Village and other Downtown neighborhoods, where most streets have names instead of numbers and run at all angles.

Security
Be prepared to pass
through security
checkpoints with
metal detectors at
such tourist
attractions as the
Statue of Liberty
and Empire State
Building.

TELEPHONE AND FAXES

Most Manhattan locations have a 212 area code, or the recently added 646. Cell phones can be 646 or 917. Brooklyn, Queens, Staten Island, and Bronx numbers are prefixed by 718 or the newer 347. The area code of the number being called must be used even within the city, always preceded by 1.

Toll-free calls are prefixed by 800, 866, 877, or 888; remember to dial 1 first when calling these numbers.

Public telephones accepting credit cards are becoming scarce, but can still be found in centers such as Grand Central Terminal and Penn Station. Hotels usually add a hefty surcharge for phone calls. Telephone dialing cards, available at convenience stores and newsstands, are an inexpensive way to make calls.

Cell Phones

Cell phone usage is widespread. Cell phones may be rented from Roberts Rent-a-Phone (tel: 800-964-2468) and Hello World (tel: 212-243-8800), but consider buying one: prices are fairly cheap compared to many other cities.

Fax

Most major hotels offer a fax service; faxes can also be sent from many copy and printing shops, as well as from the numerous branches of FedEx/Kinko's, which offer computer access for a fee.

Useful Numbers

International calls, dial 011 (the international access code), then the country code, city code, and local number.

Directory help, dial 555-1212 preceded by the area code you are calling from, or 411.

Non-Emergency Services

New York has a three-digit number to be dialed for information and non-emergency services. Calls to 311 are answered by a live operator 24 hours a day, seven days a week, and services are provided in over 170 languages. Operators are prepared to respond to a wide range of calls, including tourist inquiries, complaints about noise, queries about public transportation, and information about lost items.

TIME ZONE

New York observes Eastern Standard Time (EST). This is five hours behind London, one hour ahead of Chicago, and three hours ahead of California.

TIPPING

Most New Yorkers in the service industries (restaurants, hotels, transportation) regard tips as a God-given right, not just a pleasant gratuity. The fact is, many people rely on tips to make up for what are often poor hourly salaries. Therefore, unless service is truly horrendous, you can figure on tipping everyone from bellmen and porters (usually $1 a bag; or $2 if only one bag); to hotel doormen ($2 if they hail you a cab); hotel maids ($1–2 a day, left in your room when you check out), restroom attendants (at least 50¢), and room-service waiters (approximately 15

TV Tickets
With advance
planning, it's
possible to join the
audience of a New
York-based TV
show, many of them
shown overseas.
Tickets are often
free and sometimes
distributed by lottery.
For details, go to
www.nycitygo.com
or see the website
of your favorite
program.

percent of the bill unless already added on). In restaurants, the best way to figure out the tip is to double the tax (which adds up to a little more than 16 percent; add or subtract a dollar or two depending on how the service was). In taxis, tip 15 percent of the total fare.

TOURIST INFORMATION

NYC & Company Visitors Information Center: 810 Seventh Avenue (between West 52nd and 53rd streets); tel: 212-484-1222, 800-NYC-VISIT; www.nycgo.com; Mon–Fri 8.30am–6pm, Sat–Sun 9am–5pm. The center offers brochures, maps, and information about hotels and attraction discounts. An information kiosk is at Broadway and Park Row at City Hall Park.

Times Square Information Center: Seventh Avenue (between West 46th and 47th streets); tel: 212-768-0233; www.timessquarenyc.org; Mon–Fri 9am–7pm, Sat–Sun 8am–8pm. City info, plus Broadway show tickets.

TRANSPORTATION

Subways and Buses

Subways and buses run 24 hours a day, less frequently (and some lines not at all) after midnight. Fares are payable by exact change by MetroCard pass (available at subway ticket booths), which allows free transfers within two hours of use. Unlimited-ride passes for seven or 30 days are available, as is a day pass.

Buses run on most avenues (except Park Avenue) as well as on the following cross-streets: Houston, 14th, 23rd, 34th, 42nd, 49th–50th, 57th, 66th, 79th, 86th, 96th, 116th, and 125th.

Subway shuttle trains cross town at 14th and 42nd streets. Queens lines N and R also cross from east to west in Manhattan. There is no north–south line east of Lexington Avenue or west of Eighth Avenue and Broadway.

For bus and subway information, call: 718-330-1234, or see www.mta.info; for details about the MetroCard, call 212/800-METROCARD.

PATH Trains

PATH (Port Authority Trans Hudson) trains run under the Hudson River from Manhattan to Hoboken, Jersey City, and Newark in New Jersey. For information, call 800-234-PATH.

Rail and Bus Stations

Long-distance and commuter trains arrive and depart from Manhattan's two terminals: Grand Central at Park Avenue and 42nd Street, and Pennsylvania at Seventh Avenue and 33rd Street. For information on Amtrak, the national rail service, tel: 800-872-7245.

The city's main bus terminal is Port Authority (Eighth Avenue between 40th and 42nd streets). The station sits on two subway lines and is serviced by long-distance bus companies (including Greyhound: tel: 800-231-2222) and commuter lines. City buses stop outside.

WEIGHTS AND MEASURES

The US uses the imperial system.

Above from far left: the *Late Show* tapes at the Ed Sullivan Theater on Broadway; coin-operated binoculars on Liberty Island; the *Charging Bull* scupture at the Bowling Green in Lower Manhattan (*see p.93*); the CNN Studios are in the Time Warner Center on Columbus Circle.

Websites
www.newyork.city search.com for listings and reviews of current arts and entertainment events, as well as restaurants and shopping.
www.nyc.gov is the official site of the City of New York.
www.nycgo.com is the New York City tourism website, with information on hotels, restaurants, shopping, events, and promotions.
www.centralpark nyc.org details what's on at and all about Central Park, including maps.
www.nypl.org is for everything you ever wanted to know about the New York Public Library. There's also an online information service.

New York hotels are the most expensive in the US and you may not get much space for your money, but some recent additions have made the city a bit more affordable. The five-star properties are as luxurious as any in the world, but since tabs beginning at $600 a day are beyond many travelers, some of the top selections are listed with contact information in the margin *(opposite)*, while the listings below feature a wider range of choices. Rates vary by season, with the low periods in winter and in August, but hotel websites may have special rates and packages anytime. Many hotels offer discounts for longer stays or reservations booked well in advance. Discount websites are useful as well; quikbook.com has many New York offerings; kayak.com lets you compare several services on one site.

Midtown

414 Hotel

414 West 44th Street (between Ninth and Tenth avenues); tel: 212-399-0006, 866-414-4683; www.414hotel.com; subway: 42nd Street Eighth Avenue; $–$$

Two brownstones with a courtyard between have been transformed into a best-bet budget boutique with a location perfect for Broadway theaters.

> Price for a double room for one night without breakfast:
>
> | | |
> |---|---|
> | $$$$ | over $300 |
> | $$$ | $250–$300 |
> | $$ | $200–$250 |
> | $ | under $200 |

Distrikt Hotel

342 West 40th Street (at Ninth Avenue); tel: 212-706-6100, 888-444-5620; http://distrikthotel.com; subway: 42nd Street Broadway or Eighth Avenue; $$

A sleek boutique Theater District newcomer with a twist – each floor has a city neighbourhood theme. Amenities are luxury (Frette linens, robes, soundproof windows) but rates are not.

Hotel Metro

45 West 35th Street (between Fifth and Sixth avenues); tel: 212-947-2500; www.hotelmetronyc.com; subway: 34th Street Herald Square; $$

Popular with the fashion industry, the Metro has a Deco feel, spacious rooms that are updated regularly, and nice features like a library, rooftop terrace, and free continental breakfast.

La Quinta Manhattan

17 West 32nd Street (near Fifth Avenue); tel: 212-736-1600, 800-551-2303; www.applecorehotels.com; subway: 34th Street Herald Square; $

A short walk from Macy's or Penn Station, this comfortable chain hotel offers reasonable rates that include an on-site fitness center and free continental breakfast. Visit the open-air rooftop bar for drinks with a view in summer.

The London NYC

151 West 54th Street (between Sixth and Seventh avenues); tel: 866-690-2029; www.thelondonnyc.com; subway: 57th Street; $$$

The all-suite London boasts style and

unusually large quarters for New York, not to mention room service from the first NY outpost of London star chef Gordon Ramsay.

The Manhattan at Times Square Hotel

790 Seventh Avenue (at 51st Street); tel: 212-581-3300, 800-223-6550; www.starwood.com; subway: 50th Street, Broadway; $–$$

Because it is lesser known than its sibling, the huge Sheraton aross the street, the 22-story Manhattan often posts budget rates, even though it offers full commercial hotel services, good-sized rooms, a health club, and a large indoor pool.

Michelangelo Hotel

152 West 51st Street (just west of Seventh Avenue); tel: 212-765-1900; www.michelangelohotel.com; subway: 49th Street N or R, 50th Street 1; $$–$$$

An oasis of calm and elegance just off Broadway, this hotel offers old-world ambience and comfortable rooms at comfortable rates.

The Plaza

Fifth Avenue (at 59th Street); tel: 212-759-3000; www.theplaza.com; subway: Fifth Avenue; $$$

One of New York's grand hotels, The Plaza recently underwent a renovation that restored its Edwardian-style splendor. Rooms are furnished with antiques and adorned with murals. The Oak Bar and Edwardian Room are favorite pre- and post-theater spots.

Waldorf-Astoria

50th Street and Park Avenue; tel: 212-355-3000, 800-925-3673; www.waldorf.com; subway: 51st Street 6; $$$$

The most famous hotel in the city during its heyday in the 1930s and 1940s, with a panache that's been restored to something like its early glory. Most rooms have an old-world charm, and the location is convenient.

Wellington Hotel

871 Seventh Avenue (at 55th Street); tel: 212-247-3900, 800-652-1212; www.wellingtonhotel.com; subway: 57th Street F; $$

The side-street entrance in a congested neighborhood is useful and the location is great for Central Park, Lincoln Center, and Carnegie Hall. A reliable standby for reasonable rates.

W New York

541 Lexington Avenue (near East 49th Street); tel: 212-755-1200; www.whotels.com; subway: 51st Street 6; $$$

W's interior was designed by entertainment architect David Rockwell and features Zen-inspired rooms. There's a juice bar, a spa with good fitness facilities, and a trendsetting restaurant called Heartbeat.

Chelsea to Gramercy Park

70 Park Avenue

70 Park Avenue (at 38th Street); tel: 212-973-2400, 877-707-2752; www.70parkave.com: subway Grand Central; $–$$

Above from far left: Hotel Chelsea; the lobby of the Waldorf-Astoria.

Five-Star Hotels
For those who can afford the tab – way upwards of $500 per day – these top New York properties offer ultimate luxury: Four Seasons (57 East 57th Street between Park and Madison avenues; tel: 212-758-5700; www. fourseasons.com); Mandarin Oriental (80 Columbus Circle at 60th Street; tel: 212-805-8800, 866-801-8880; www. mandarinoriental. com); Pierre (2 East 61st Street at Fifth Avenue; tel: 212-838-8000; www.taj hotels.com); St Regis (2 East 55th Street at Fifth Avenue; tel: 212-753-4500; www. stregis.com); Trump International, 1 Central Park West at Columbus Circle); tel: 212-299-1000, 800-44-TRUMP; www.trumpintl).

Lodging Tax
Added to your hotel bill are city and state taxes of 13$\frac{1}{2}$ percent plus a room charge of $2 per night.

Reasonable rates are a nice surprise at this classy Park Avenue boutique hotel that feels almost like your own pied-à-terre. Rooms are well appointed, and there's a complimentary wine reception in the lobby every night.

Gramercy Park Hotel

2 Lexington Avenue (at Gramercy Park); tel: 212-920-3300; www.gramercyparkhotel.com; subway: 23rd Street 6; $$$$

Once a faded relic from the Jazz Age, this property was brought back to life as a swank boutique hotel adorned with rich velvets, modern art, and chandeliers. The Rose and Jade bars are favorite celebrity hangouts.

Hotel Chelsea

222 West 23rd Street (near Seventh Avenue); tel: 212-243-3700; www.hotelchelsea.com; subway: 23rd Street 1; $$

A red-brick landmark of bohemian decadence, home to Beat poets, Warhol drag queens, Sid Vicious, and now… a few of all of the above plus 'ordinary' guests. Rooms are not in great shape, but those who dig the vibe don't seem to mind. Currently up for sale; keep an eye on the website for developments.

Inn at Irving Place

56 Irving Place (near East 18th Street); tel: 212-533-4600, 800-685-1447; www.innatirving.com; subway: 23rd Street 6; $$$$

This pair of graceful townhouses have been transformed into a facsimile of a country inn, with a cozy fireplace-lit tea salon and 12 elegant rooms and suites featuring four-poster beds. There's a nice little restaurant on the lower level that offers room service.

Upper West Side

Beacon Hotel

2130 Broadway (between 74th and 75th streets); tel: 212-787-1100, 800-572-4969; www.beaconhotel.com; subway: 72nd Street Broadway; $$

Newly decorated, with good-sized rooms and a convenient location, the unpretentious Beacon is a good choice, especially if you are a fan of the groups playing at the Beacon Theater, the musical landmark next door.

Lucerne Hotel

201 West 79th Street (at Amsterdam Avenue); tel: 212-875-1000, 800-492-8122; www.thelucernehotel.com; subway: 79th Street; $$$

A 1904 landmark building has become the gracious Lucerne, with European-inspired decor and many amenities. The hotel's Nice Matin restaurant is a favourite in the neighborhood.

Marakech Hotel

2688 Broadway (at West 103rd Street); tel: 212-663-0275; subway: 103 Street 1; $

Price for a double room for one night without breakfast:

$$$$	over $300
$$$	$250–$300
$$	$200–$250
$	under $200

Recently redone with colourful Moroccan decor, this definitely remains a budget spot with very small rooms, but has upgraded with amenities including all private baths, flat-screen TV, and massage shower heads. There's a café, lounge, and a Starbucks on the premises.

On The Ave Hotel

2178 Broadway (at 77th Street); tel: 212-362-1100, 800-509-7598; www.ontheave-nyc.com; subway: 79th Street 1; $$$

The hotel offers stylish rooms. It is within walking distance of the American Museum of Natural History and prime Upper West Side shopping.

Upper East Side

The Carlyle

35 East 76th Street (at Madison Avenue); tel: 212-744-1600, 800-227-5737; www.thecarlyle.com; subway: 77th Street 6; $$$$

Posh, reserved, and serene, the Carlyle remains a highly acclaimed luxury hotel. The appointments are exquisite, the furnishings antique, the service formal. The hotel is the home of Café Carlyle and Bemelmans Bar, two of the city's most enduring upscale evening spots.

The Franklin

164 East 87th Street (between Lexington and Third avenues); tel: 212-369-1000, 877-847-4444; www.franklinhotel.com; subway: 86th Street 4, 5, 6; $$$

This boutique hotel has upgraded and is not the bargain it once was, but look out for special rates. Despite very small rooms, the atmosphere is charming, the complimentary breakfast delicious, the beds heavenly. Guests enjoy WiFi access, nightly wine and cheese reception, 24-hour cappuccino and espresso.

Gracie Inn

502 East 81st Street (at York Avenue); tel: 212-628-1700, 800-404-2252; www.thegracieinn.com; subway: 77th Street 6; $$

On a side street in a quiet part of town near Gracie Mansion (the mayor's official residence), this place is a cross between a townhouse and a country inn. From small studios to large penthouses, rates are subject to reduction depending on the length of your stay.

Hotel Wales

1295 Madison Avenue (at 92nd Street); tel: 212-876-6000, 800-428-5252; www.waleshotel.com; subway: 96th Street 6; $$$

The Wales offers a great location in Carnegie Hill, near Museum Mile and Central Park. Feast on the city's best breakfast next door at Sarabeth's Kitchen, or enjoy the light one offered in the hotel's tea salon, also the setting for afternoon tea and chamber music.

The Lowell

28 East 63rd Street (at Madison Avenue); tel: 212-838-1400; www.lowellhotel.com; subway: Lexington Avenue 63rd Street; $$$$

Understated elegance is the byword at this exclusive, polished all-suite property just off chic Madison Avenue. The hotel is known for its elegant tea salon.

Above from far left: boutique chic at The Franklin; a suite with a stunning view at The Carlyle.

Student Hostels
Students and other budget travelers might consider staying at one of several hostels. Most offer dorm-style lodging, shared bathrooms, and a common kitchen for a fraction of the cost of a standard hotel. Manhattan locations include Big Apple Hostel (119 West 45th Street; tel: 212-302-2603); Chelsea International Hostel (251 West 20th Street; tel: 212-243-7700); and HI-New York (891 Amsterdam Avenue; tel: 212-932-2300).

B&Bs
Bed and breakfast accommodations in New York range from a room in someone's apartment to a full apartment or small inn. For information, contact City Lights (tel: 212-737-7049; www.citylights newyork.com) or Bed and Breakfast Network of New York (tel: 212-645-8134, 800-900-8134; http://bedand breakfastnetny.com).

The Mark
Madison Avenue at 77th Street; tel: 212-744-4300, 866-744-4300; www.themarkhotel.com; subway: 77th Street; $$$$

Fresh from a total makeover at its prestigious Upper East Side address, The Mark is a model of contemporary luxury, and boasts a celebrity chef since Jean-Georges Vongerichten came aboard in 2010. Special offers on the hotel website make it more affordable.

Greenwich Village and the Meatpacking District

Abingdon Guest House
13 Eighth Avenue (between West 12th and Jane streets); tel: 212-243-5384; www.abingdonguesthouse.com; subway: Eighth Avenue 14th Street; $$

It's romance on a shoestring at this nine-room hostelry between the West Village and the Meatpacking District. Divided between two townhouses, each of the tiny rooms is individually decorated: some have four-poster beds. The rooms facing Eighth Avenue can be noisy, so ask for the Garden Room in the back. A two-night minimum stay may be required on weekends and holidays.

Hotel Gansevoort
18 Ninth Avenue (at 13th Street); tel: 212-206-6700, 877-426-7386; www.hotelgansevoort.com; subway: Eighth Avenue 14th Street; $$$$

The Meatpacking District's first luxury hotel has a rooftop bar, swimming pool, and breathtaking views. Bedrooms are fashionably appointed (think neutral colors and a single orchid). If your room faces west, the Hudson River will be on the horizon and the Meatpacking action will be taking place directly below, nonstop.

The Jane
113 Jane Street (at West Street); tel: 212-924-6700; www.thejanenyc.com; subway: Eighth Avenue 14th Street; $–$$

A new incarnation of a budget hotel in a 1907 seaman's home, The Jane has carefully kept the quirky nostalgia while modernizing. Compact rooms are reminiscent of seamen's bunks. All have private baths, some offer river views and terraces. It's a bit of a walk to public transportation, but it is surrounded by some of the city's prettiest blocks.

Washington Square Hotel
103 Waverly Place (near Macdougal Street); tel: 212-777-9515; www.washingtonsquarehotel.com; subway: West Fourth Street; $

A century-old hotel that offers an ideal Village location on Washington Square Park. The rooms are small but nicely appointed. In a former incarnation, this was the seedy Hotel Earle, where Papa John Phillips of the 1960s folk group The Mamas & the Papas wrote the folk-rock classic 'California Dreaming.'

Price for a double room for one night without breakfast:	
$$$$	over $300
$$$	$250–$300
$$	$200–$250
$	under $200

Soho and Tribeca

Duane Street Hotel

130 Duane Street (near Church Street); tel: 800-916-8592, www. duanestreethotel.com; subway: Chamber Street, A, C; $$–$$$

This small, sleek new contemporary hotel offers moderate rates in a pricey neighbourhood.

Greenwich Hotel

377 Greenwich Street (near Moore Street); tel: 212-941-8900; www.the greenwichhotel.com; subway: Franklin Street; $$$$

Robert De Niro and partners planned this exceptional luxury hotel with a residential feel. It offers a warm sitting room with fireplace and a landscaped courtyard, extra-spacious guest rooms, and an indoor pool. Rustic-elegant decor mixes Tibetan rugs, Moroccan and Italian tiles, old wood beams, and Asian antiques.

Mercer Hotel

147 Mercer Street (near Prince Street); tel: 212-966-6060, 888-918-6060; www.mercerhotel.com; subway: Prince Street; $$$$

This 1890s landmark has 75 rooms with high loft ceilings, WiFi access, flat-screen televisions, and (for New York) spacious bathrooms. Andre Balazs, the owner, also owns Chateau Marmont in Los Angeles, and the clientele here is equally stylish and high profile. Facilities include a roof garden, a library bar with 24-hour service, complimentary gym access, and the highly regarded Mercer Kitchen restaurant and café.

SoHo Grand

310 W. Broadway (near Canal Street); tel: 212-965-3000, 877-965-3236; www.sohogrand.com; subway: Canal Street A, C, E; $$$$

Expect excellent service at this 15-story hotel, with industrial-chic decor and magnificent upper-floor views. Rooms have large windows. The lobby and bar are the rendezvous of choice for cool media types and rock stars.

Lower East Side

Hotel on Rivington

107 Rivington Street (near Ludlow Street); tel: 212-475-2600; www.hotelonrivington.com; subway: Delancy Street; $$$$

This sleek glass-walled hotel is bringing a dash of contemporary style to the gentrifying Lower East Side.

Lower Manhattan

Best Western Seaport Inn

33 Peck Slip (at Front Street); tel: 212-766-6600, 800-HOTEL-NY; www.bestwestern.com; subway: Fulton Street 2, 3; $$

This converted 19th-century warehouse has 72 rooms with Federal-style furnishings. Some rooms have views of the Brooklyn Bridge.

Holiday Inn Wall Street

15 Gold Street (at Platt Street); tel: 212-232-7700, 800-HOLIDAY; www.holidayinn.com; subway: Fulton Street 2, 3; $$

Business and pleasure meet here, with high-speed internet and work stations in every room as well as homey touches.

Above from far left: the Mercer Hotel in Soho; the Lower East Side's Hotel on Rivington.

Helping Hand
Few people are more useful to first-time visitors than a knowledgeable concierge. Searching for a romantic bistro, a hip nightclub, or hard-to-get theater tickets? A good concierge will be able to help you out.

Blue Fin

W Times Square Hotel, 1567 Broadway (between 46th and 47th streets); tel: 212-918-1400; daily B, L, and D; subway: 49th Street N, R, W; $$$

It's easy to be swept away by this seafood restaurant's over-the-top decor; in the street-level bar only a glass wall separates diners from the hubbub of Times Square, and Austin Powers would feel at home in the retro dining room. The sushi is sublime, and 'cooked' dishes such as sesame-crusted tuna and pan-roasted bass are a close second.

Convivio

45 Tudor City Place (42nd Street between First and Second avenues); tel: 212-599-5045; Mon–Fri L and D, Sat, Sun D; subway: 42nd Street; $$$$

Tucked away in Tudor City, this serene southern Italian with a Michelin star is good value among the city's fine dining choices, especially the four-course *prix-fixe* menu. Expect traditional pastas and dishes such as lamb, veal, or wild bass, to be done with flair.

Four Seasons

99 East 52nd Street (between Lexington and Park avenues); tel: 212-754 9494; Mon–Fri L and D, Sat D only; subway: Lexington Avenue/51st Street; $$$$

Since it opened nearly 50 years ago, the Four Seasons in the landmark Seagram Building has had a clientele to rival any Who's Who listing. The decor is priceless *(see p.45)* and the seasonal classics served are impeccable.

La Bonne Soupe

48 West 55th Street (between Fifth and Sixth avenues); tel: 212-586-7650; daily L and D; subway: N, R, or F to 57th Street; $–$$

When cash is low, head for this old-time French bistro, a standby since 1973 for crepes, quiche, fondues, and great onion soup as well as *steak frites* and *poulet*. Reserve ahead or be prepared to stand in line.

La Grenouille

3 East 52nd Street (between Fifth and Madison avenues); tel: 212-752 1495; Mon D, Tue–Sat L and D; subway: Fifth Avenue/53rd Street; $$$$

One of the last of the great French eateries in Midtown, where a quenelle is still a quenelle and the flowers have rarely been more beautiful. A classic.

Smith & Wollensky

797 Third Avenue (49th Street); tel: 212-753-1530; daily L and D; subway: 51st Street 6; $$$

This New York institution is usually packed with stockbrokers and Midtown executives, who come for the great steaks, extensive American wine list, and clubby, masculine atmosphere.

Price guide for a three-course dinner for one:	
$$$$	over $70
$$$	$50–70
$$	$25–50
$	under $25

The adjacent Wollensky's Grill is more casual and a bit less expensive.

Trattoria Dell'Arte

900 Seventh Avenue (at 56th Street); tel: 212-245-9800; daily L and D; subway: 57th Street/Seventh Avenue; $$$

The fabulous antipasto bar doubles as a main course at this popular trattoria near Carnegie hall. The seafood, pasta, and gourmet pizza are good choices, too.

Upper West Side

Dallas BBQ

27 West 72nd Street (between Central Park West and Columbus Avenue); tel: 212-873-2004; daily L and D; 72nd Street B, C; $

It isn't gourmet, but this barbecue joint is always crowded. The reason: chicken and ribs platters (with side dishes) for under $12.

Gray's Papaya

2090 Broadway (at 72nd Street); tel: 212-799-0243; daily 24 hours; 72nd Street 1, 2, 3, 9; $

A two hot-dog dinner with a fruit-juice chaser. Stand-up only. Whaddaya expect for three bucks?

Jean-Georges

Trump International Hotel, 1 Central Park West; tel: 212-299-3900; Mon–Sat L and D, Sun Br; subway: Columbus Circle; $$–$$$$

The skyscraper on chaotic Columbus Circle is an unlikely location for one of the city's most sophisticated and relaxing retreats. Chef Jean-Georges Vongerichten delights diners with creative versions of French classics. The bill can soar as high as the building, but the *prix-fixe* lunch at the adjoining Nougatine brings these gastronomic heights within reach. Book ahead.

La Boite en Bois

75 West 68th Street (between Columbus Avenue and Central Park West); tel: 212-874-2705; daily L and D; 72nd Street B,C; $$–$$$

A standby near Lincoln Center for 25 years, this tiny bistro serves authentic French fare. The three-course, pre-theater *prix-fixe* menu is good value.

Upper East Side

Beyoglu

1431 Third Avenue (at 81st Street), 2nd floor; tel: 212-650-0850; daily D; subway: 77th Street 6; $$

Middle Eastern flavors burst from dishes such as yogurt rice soup, lamb kebab, hummus, and sauteed eggplant at this meze restaurant named after an Istanbul neighborhood. The portions are ideal for sharing, so come with a group and explore the whole menu.

Daniel

60 East 65th Street (near Park Avenue); tel: 212-288-0033; Mon–Sat D; subway: Lexington Avenue/63rd Street; $$$$

Master chef Daniel Boulud presides over this expensive food kingdom, but gourmets will gladly spend for the unique quality and service he delivers. The cuisine is mostly French with a few unexpected (but not gimmicky) twists, and the service is impeccable.

Above from far left: the grill room in the Four Seasons; al fresco drinks in Greenwich Village.

Café Culture
In New York, 'café' refers to a wide variety of places. Some are full-fledged restaurants; others are little more than a take-out counter and a table or two. Some have European flair; others are more akin to traditional American diners. Unsurprisingly, Starbucks are ubiquitous. There are no fewer than 90 in Midtown alone.

Sweet Dreams

Few places in New York can satisfy an ice-cream craving as lavishly as Serendipity 3 on East 60th Street between Second and Third avenues. The frozen hot chocolate and huge banana splits are legendary. Kids and shoppers from nearby Bloomingdale's crowd in by day, clubbers stop by at night; and no one seems to mind the cranky service or grown-up tabs.

L'Absinthe

227 East 67th Street (between Second and Third avenues); tel: 212-794-4950; Mon–Sat L and D, Sun Br and D; subway: 68th Street/Hunter College; $$$

The etched mirrors, polished brass, and French waiters in white aprons are as authentic as the classic brasserie fare.

Spigolo

1561 Second Avenue (at 81st Street); tel: 212-744-1100; daily D; subway: 77th Street; $$$

A husband-wife team trained at Union Square Café have created a tiny gem widely recognized for exceptional Italian fare. Reserve well in advance.

Chelsea to Gramercy Park

Cookshop

156 Tenth Avenue (at 20th Street); tel: 212-924-4440; daily L and D, Mon–Fri B; subway 23rd Street; $–$$

Support from local farmers means the freshest ingredients at this unpretentious Chelsea spot with good American food. Weekend brunches are wildly popular.

Friend of a Farmer

77 Irving Place (between 18th and 19th streets); tel: 212-477-2188; Mon–Fri B, L, and D, Sat–Sun Br and D; subway: Union Square; $$

It feels like a Vermont inn at this cozy restaurant serving hearty portions of American fare. Great for families.

Gramercy Tavern

42 East 20th Street (between Broadway and Park Avenue); tel: 212-477-0777; Mon–Fri L, daily D; subway: Union Square; $$$$

The Gramercy's New American cuisine is artfully prepared, and the handsome dining room has a homey feeling. Be sure to leave room for the chocolate bread pudding.

Half King

505 West 23rd Street (at Tenth Avenue); tel: 212-462-4300; Mon–Fri B, L, and D, Sat–Sun Br and D; 23rd Street C, E; $

Just the sort of easygoing place that Chelsea could use more of. The bar and dining room serve as a gallery for artists and photojournalists, and the garden is a snug retreat. The fish and chips, shepherd's pie, burgers, and other pub fare are fairly priced.

Novità

102 East 22nd Street (between Park and Lexington avenues); tel: 212-677-2222; daily L and D; 23rd Street 6; $$$

This northern Italian restaurant remains an undiscovered gem. Expect delicious, freshly prepared dishes, gracious service, and reasonable prices.

Union Square Café

21 East 16th Street (between Fifth Avenue and Union Square); tel: 212-243-4020; daily L and D; subway: Union Square; $$$$

A winning formula of top-flight food and service makes this a favorite of residents and tourists alike. The atmosphere is casual, but in a studied way. The chefs make full use of local ingredients sold by farmers at Union

Square's Greenmarket to create a menu of mostly American fare, with a distinctly Italian accent.

Greenwich Village and the Meatpacking District

Blue Hill

75 Washington Place (between Sixth Avenue and Washington Square West); tel: 212-539-1776; daily D; subway: West 4th Street; $$$$

A mellow, sophisticated spot that gets rave reviews for beautifully conceived American dishes made with fresh ingredients from the Blue Hill family farm.

CamaJe

85 Macdougal Street (between Bleecker and Houston streets); tel: 212-673-8184; daily L and D; subway: West Fourth Street; $–$$

Chef Abigail Hitchcock prepares top-notch French bistro dishes with imagination and heart. The casual atmosphere and reasonable prices make this a real find.

Da Silvano

260 Sixth Avenue (between Bleecker and Houston streets); tel: 212-982-2343; daily L and D; subway: Houston Street; $$$

Simple, flavorful Tuscan cuisine attracts

a loyal following, including quite a few celebrities. A less expensive option is next door at Bar Pitti, run by the same folks, with similar Tuscan tastes.

Del Posto

85 Tenth Avenue (between 15th and 16th streets); tel: 212-497-8090; Mon–Fri L and D, Sat–Sun D; subway, 14th Street/Eighth Avenue; $$$

Mario Batali's most ambitious show-place on the edge of the Meatpacking District lives up to its palazzo feel, with Italian food that reviewers have called 'heavenly.' Despite the formal setting, the staff is friendly and the piano music relaxing. The Italian wine list is enormous.

Mexicana Mama

525 Hudson Street (between Charles and West 10th streets); tel: 212-924-4119; Tue–Sun L and D; subway: Christopher Street/Sheridan Square; $$

This tiny Mexican spot is worth the wait to get in. The menu is limited, but the boldly flavored dishes are a far cry from average Tex-Mex fare. A taco here is a culinary masterpiece. Cash only.

Pearl Oyster Bar

18 Cornelia Street (between Bleecker and West Fourth streets); tel: 212-691-8211; Mon–Fri L and D, Sat D; subway: West Fourth Street; $$

This raw bar is tucked into a side street populated by other small restaurants. Chowder is served, in addition to what some call 'perfection on the half-shell.'

Above from far left: placing an order at a New York café; Gramercy Tavern; a Lower East Side café; Pearl Oyster Bar.

Price guide for a three-course dinner for one:	
$$$$	over $70
$$$	$50–70
$$	$25–50
$	under $25

Beard's Best

The James Beard House at 167 West 12th Street (at Seventh Avenue) is now a club for food enthusiasts who enjoy meals cooked by established and emerging chefs from around the world. Beard, considered the father of American gastronomy, died in 1985.

Spice Market

403 West 13th Street (at Ninth Avenue); tel: 212-675-2322; daily Br, L, and D; subway: 14th Street/ Eighth Avenue; $$

Celebrity chef Jean-Georges Vongerichten oversees a spicy menu inspired by Asian street fare at this stylish, two-floor warehouse space.

The Spotted Pig

314 West 11th Street (at Greenwich Street); tel: 212-620-0393; daily L and D; subway: Christopher Street/ Sheridan Square; $$

Another popular entry in Mario Batali's Manhattan empire, this tiny, casual restaurant elevates pub food to gourmet status. Sit on plump cushions at small tables or perch on a stool and dig into chicken liver parfait, squid and mussel salad, or slow-braised beef shin with risotto. For a calmer scene, visit at lunch.

East Village, Little Italy, and Lower East Side

I Coppi

432 East 9th Street (between First Avenue and Avenue A); tel: 212-254-2263; Mon–Fri D, Sat–Sun Br and D; subway: First Avenue; $$$

This casual Italian restaurant oozes authenticity thanks to brick walls, terracotta floors, a wood-burning oven, and a pretty back garden. Expect the full-bodied cooking of rural Tuscany.

Puglia

189 Hester Street (at Mulberry Street); tel: 212-966-6006; daily L and D; subway: Canal Street J, M, Z; $$

The Little Italy of old has persisted here since 1919. Things get 'pretty crazy' at night, according to the manager Joey, but group tables, a singer called 'The Fat Lady,' plus lots of red sauce and red wine make it a party every night.

Rice

292 Elizabeth Street (at East Houston Street); tel: 212-226-5775; subway: Broadway/Lafayette Street; daily L and D; $

The menu at this hipster haven consists of about 10 varieties of rice (including Bhutanese red, Thai black, and Japanese short), served with a choice of toppings: ratatouille, curries, lemongrass chicken salad, and the like. Finish with rice-crispy treats or rice pudding.

Soho

Bread

20 Spring Street (near Elizabeth Street); tel: 212-334-1015; daily L and D; subway: Spring Street 6; $

This tiny café and wine bar celebrates bread and all that can go between it. Hot panini are filled with everything from pesto chicken, avocado, and goat's cheese to shiitake mushrooms, fresh sardines, and tomatoes. There are salads and pastas as well.

Jane

100 West Houston Street (near Thompson Street); tel: 212-254-7000; Mon–Sat L, daily D, Sun Br; subway: Houston Street or Spring Street; $$

There's nothing plain about this Jane,

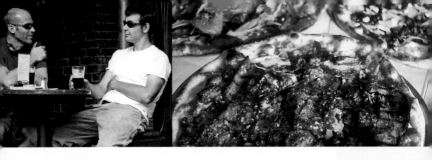

where creative American dishes such as honey-braised pork and grilled sirloin are crafted from fresh, locally grown ingredients. Be sure to leave room for dessert.

Savoy

70 Prince Street (at Crosby Street); tel: 212-219-8570; Mon–Sat L, daily D; subway: Prince Street or Spring Street; $$–$$$

Only the freshest local ingredients go into the seasonal Med-New American menus at this SoHo standby. The setting is an 1830s brownstone, made cozy in winter by a wood-burning fireplace.

Tribeca

Bouley

120 West Broadway (at Duane Street); tel: 212-964-2525; daily L and D; subway: Chambers Street 1, 2, 3; $$$$

Fans claim that experiencing David Bouley's 'new French' food transcends price. Perhaps a better way to put it is that eating at this elegantly hip restaurant is, at its best, a transcendent culinary experience… if you can afford it.

Bubby's

120 Hudson Street (at North Moore Street); tel: 212-219-0666; daily B, L, and D; subway: Franklin Street; $

This place feels like a farmhouse kitchen transplanted into the city. Every order comes with a basket of biscuits, and the menu boasts 'food like Mom would make if she only knew how.' Under-eights eat free on Sunday night.

Nobu

105 Hudson Street (between Franklin and North Moore streets); tel: 212-219-0500; Mon–Fri L, daily D; subway: Franklin Street; $$$$

Celebrity-spotting is a favorite pastime at this Tribeca hotspot, justly acclaimed for chef Nobu Matsuhisa's Japanese-Peruvian cuisine. It is virtually impossible to book a reservation, but Nobu Next Door (no reservations accepted) is a good second choice.

Lower Manhattan

Delmonico's

56 Beaver Street (at William Street); tel: 212-509-1144; Mon–Fri L and D; subway: Wall Street 2, 3; $$$$

Wall Street deal-makers congregate at this clubby, chummy, old-time steakhouse. Beef is the specialty, of course, but the lobster, oysters Rockefeller, and other seafood dishes are quite good, too.

Gigino at Wagner Park

20 Battery Place (at West Street); tel: 212-528-2228; daily L and D; subway: Bowling Green; $$

With sunset views of the Statue of Liberty, this moderately priced Italian could easily pander to tourists, but the food is high-quality and creative. When the weather is fine, the terrace is irresistible.

Above from far left: Bread; Bubby's; cool drinks in the West Village; head to Little Italy for gourmet pizza.

Cup o' Joe
If you ask for 'regular coffee' in New York, you'll most likely get American coffee with cream and sugar. If you don't take anything in your coffee, ask for 'black coffee.'

Price guide for a three-course dinner for one:	
$$$$	over $70
$$$	$50–70
$$	$25–50
$	under $25

The opportunities for entertainment and nightlife in New York could provide different diversions 365 days a year. This is a selection of some of the key venues.

Theater

Broadway

New York's Theater District is home to 40 active theaters, most on the side streets off Broadway, spanning Sixth to Eighth avenues between 41st and 53rd streets. For a list of current shows and theaters, see www.ilovenytheater.com.

Lincoln Center Theater

150 West 65th Street between Broadway and Amsterdam Avenue; tel: 212-239-6200; www.lct.org

The 1080-seat Vivian Beaumont and the 299-seat Newhouse, Lincoln Center stage both large-scale and intimate musical and dramatic plays.

Manhattan Theatre Club

Samuel Friedman Theater, 261 West 47th Street, tel: 212-239-6200; Stage 1, New York City Center, 131 West 55th Street; tel: 212-581-1212; www.manhattantheatreclub.org

Founded in 1970, this company produces many notable plays, including American premieres of works by playwrights such as Alan Ayckbourn.

Public Theater

425 Lafayette Street (between East 4th Street and Astor Place); tel: 212-539-8500; www.publictheater.org

Founded as the Shakespeare Workshop and still sponsors of free Shakespeare in the Park, the Public has grown into a showcase for the new and experimental. *Hair* and *A Chorus Line* were born here.

Roundabout Theatre Company

Tel: 212-719-1300; www.roundabouttheatre.org

The city's largest repertory company with 40,000 subscribers, three theaters, and countless awards, the Roundabout was founded in 1965 to revive classics. It later expanded to include new works.

Music and Dance

Bowery Ballroom

6 Delancey Street (between Bowery and Christie streets); tel: 212-533-2111; www.boweryballroom.com

The 'in' spot to hear the best bands in concert, including top indie-rock bands.

Brooklyn Academy of Museum

30 Lafayette Avenue, Brooklyn; tel: 718-636-4100; www.bam.org

Best known as BAM, the city's oldest performing arts center is also the most progressive, offering avant-garde companies in dance, music, opera, and theater. Easy to reach by subway or the BAMbus serving Manhattan.

Carnegie Hall

57th Street (at Seventh Avenue); tel: 212-247-7800; www.carnegiehall.org

Famed for its acoustics since its opening in 1891, this landmark concert hall seating 2,800 presents the world's top musicians and orchestras, from classical to jazz.

Summer Freebies
Summer brings free Shakespeare, opera, and popular music concerts in Central Park, free music and outdoor movies in many city parks.

Jazz at Lincoln Center

23 West 60th Street, Time Warner Center; tel: 212-258-9800; www.jalc.org

This showcase for jazz high atop the Time Warner Center, opened in 2004, includes the 1,233-seat Rose Theater for concerts and the Jazz Hall of Fame. The Allen Room for cabaret and Dizzy's Club Coca-Cola, a jazz club, feature walls of glass framing city lights.

Lincoln Center

Broadway (between 63rd and 65th streets); schedules and tickets for all except Metropolitan Opera, tel: 212-721-6500; opera tickets, tel: 212-362-2000; www.lincolncenter.org

The city's cultural hub is home to the Metropolitan Opera House; the New York City Opera and the New York City Ballet at the David Koch Theater; the New York Philharmonic Orchestra at Avery Fisher Hall; the Chamber Music Society of Lincoln Cente; and the Juilliard School of Music.

New York City Center

West 55th Street (between Sixth and Seventh avenues); tel: 212-581-1212; www.nycitycenter.org

This 1923 building was Manhattan's first performing arts center, and the 2,730-seat auditorium hosts dance companies like Paul Taylor and Alvin Ailey, as well as the much-loved Encores series, revivals of vintage musicals.

Nightlife

Bemelmans Bar

The Carlyle, 35 East 76th Street and Madison Avenue; tel: 212-744-1600; www.thecarlyle.com

Charming Bemelmans murals are the backdrop at this upscale gem offering the best in jazz combos, piano, and song.

Cielo

18 West Little 12th Street; tel: 212-645-570; www.cieloclub.com

Meat Packing District clubs come and go, but Cielo seems to stay on top, with the best DJs and loyal fans packing the sunken dance floor.

Joe's Pub

425 Lafayette Street, Public Theater (see opposite); tel: 212-539-8778; www.joespub.com

Cabaret, jazz, rock, poetry – eclectic shows are always excellent here, the atmosphere is intimate, and you can order drinks and dinner to enjoy during the show.

Pacha

618 West 46th Street (between Eleventh and Twelfth avenues); tel: 212-209-7500; www.pachanyc.com

Glamour abounds at this far west side club with four levels, state-of-the-art lighting and top spinners. A happening scene.

SOB's

204 Varick Street (between Hudson Street and Sixth Avenue); tel: 243-4940; www.sobs.com

Sounds of Brazil are only the start. Reggae to blues or hip hop might be on at this lively club, which also offers dinner and dancing.

Above from far left: the world-famous Carnegie Hall; live jazz; you will never go thirsty in New York; the cultural behemoth that is the Lincoln Center.

Rooftop Bars

There's nothing more romantic in New York than a drink in a rooftop setting with the city as a backdrop. Some outdoor options include: Rooftop at the Empire Hotel (44 West 63rd Street; tel: 212-265-7400; www.empire hotelnyc.com/eat-rooftop.php); 230 Fifth (230 Fifth Avenue at 27th Street; tel: 212-725-4300; www. 230-Fifth.com). For weatherproof views, Top of The Tower (26th floor, Beekman Tower Hotel, 49th Street and First Avenue; tel: 212-980-4796; www.thebeekman hotel.com).

CREDITS

Insight Step by Step New York
Written by: John Gattuso
Updated by: Eleanor Berman
Commissioned by: Tom Stainer
Series Editor: Sarah Sweeney
Cartography Editor: James Macdonald
Picture Manager: Steven Lawrence
Art Editors: Ian Spick & Richard Cooke
Production: Tynan Dean

Photography by: Apa: Abe Nowitz, Britta Jaschinski, Anna Mockford and Nick Bonetti, Mark Read and Tony Perrottet; except: Danny Clifford/Alamy 8–9, 122tl&tr, 123tr; courtesy of American Museum of Natural History 60b, Beckett/AMNH 57br, Chesek/amnh 57mr, Finni/AMNH 59tl, br; The Brooklyn Museum of Art/Central Photo Archive 95tl; Katz-Laif/Camerapress 55tr; courtesy of the Carlyle Hotel 115; Allie Caulfield 35tr; Corbis 35tl, 78b; Doug Corrance 39br3; EveryNight Images 21tl; courtesy of The Frick Collection 55br; Fotolia 123tl; Getty Images 21tr; Bob Gruen 45br1; courtesy of The Solomon R. Guggenheim Foundation, NY/David Heald 52tr; Tony Halliday 29; Chris Huggins 42tr; Catherine Karnow 93m; courtesy of the Library of Congress 76; courtesy of the Lower East Side Tenement Museum 87; courtesy of The Metropolitan Museum of Art 48tl, 49tl, 49br, 68bl, 69tr; courtesy of Museum of the City of New York 51; courtesy of Museum of Modern Art 32tl, 33br; courtesy of New York Botanical Garden/Joseph de Sciose 96tr; courtesy of the New York City Ballet 7br; courtesy of the New York Public Library 20bl2; Keiko Niwa 89; PA/epa 21bl2; Clare Peel 37tr, 95tr, 114; Photolibrary.com 74br; courtesy of the Project for Public Spaces 50bl; courtesy Perfomance Space 122 86m; Redferns 78tr; courtesy of the Rockefeller Archive Center 35mr; MOMA, New York/Scala, Florence 33tl, 36tr; Topfoto 7ml, 90t; courtesy of Tribeca Grand Hotel 104b; courtesy of Waldorf-Astoria Hotel 43t; courtesy of Whitney Museum of American Art 41tl

Cover: Corbis (main image, front); iStockphoto (small images, front); Fotolia (back)

Printed by: CTPS-China.

© 2011 Apa Publications (UK) Limited
All rights reserved

Second Edition 2011

No part of this book may be reproduced, stored in a retrieval system or transmitted in any form or by any means (electronic, mechanical, photo-copying, recording or otherwise), without prior written permission of Apa Publications. Brief text quotations with use of photographs are exempted for book review purposes only. Information has been obtained from sources believed to be reliable, but its accuracy and completeness, and the opinions based thereon, are not guaranteed.

Although Insight Guides and the authors of this book have taken all reasonable care in preparing it, we make no warranty about the accuracy or completeness of its content, and, to the maximum extent permitted, disclaim all liability arising from its use.

www.insightguides.com

DISTRIBUTION

Worldwide
**APA Publications GmbH & Co. Verlag KG
(Singapore branch)**
7030 Ang Mo Kio Ave 5
08-65 Northstar @ AMK, Singapore 569880
Email: apasin@singnet.com.sg

UK and Ireland
GeoCenter International Ltd
Meridian House, Churchill Way West
Basingstoke, Hampshire RG21 6YR
Email: sales@geocenter.co.uk

US
Ingram Publisher Services
One Ingram Blvd, PO Box 3006
La Vergne, TN 37086-1986
Email: customer.service@ingrampublisher
services.com

Australia
Universal Publishers
PO Box 307
St. Leonards NSW 1590
Email: sales@universalpublishers.com.au

New Zealand
Hema Maps New Zealand Ltd (HNZ)
Unit 2
10 Cryers Road
East Tamaki
Auckland 2013
Email: sales.hema@clear.net.nz

CONTACTING THE EDITORS

We would appreciate it if readers would alert us
to errors or outdated information by writing to
us at insight@apaguide.co.uk or Apa Publications,
PO Box 7910, London SE1 1WE, UK.

INDEX